PRAISE
I SEE YOUR FACE BEFORE ME

This book tells the story of the lawsuit against the infamous Willowbrook State School (Staten Island, N.Y.)— how the case came to be filed and how it helped set in motion a revolution in the care of children and adults with severe mental and physical impairments. More than that, much more, it tells the story of Murray Schneps, a tenacious New York lawyer whose anger and courage were at the heart of the Willowbrook case; and of his beautiful daughter Lara, whose problems were very severe but who brought a special love and joy to the family that most others will never know. Lara truly inspired a revolution. The story of those years, and the memories that still live on, are recounted by Murray Schneps with clarity, passion, and humor, and always an unflinching honesty. From the beginning, Murray would not accept what society had in store for his daughter, and in fighting for something better, he began a lonely struggle that became a movement and that changed the world for Lara and countless others. In the end, though, it would be the life he made for Lara, and what she meant to him, that he would remember the most.

– Michael S. Lottman, Esq. - 1972–1975 Attorney for Civil Rights Division, United State Justice Department in the Willowbrook Class Action; Member of the Willowbrook Review Panel; Attorney in Private Practice handling civil rights and constitutional cases

The Willowbrook case changed the way the nation treats mentally retarded people. The case would not have happened and would not have been as successful without the intelligence and persistence of Murray Schneps. Here, Murray recites many of the stories of that case with vivid descriptions of the issues and the people involved. But maybe more importantly, Murray's daughter is at the center of this story, and Murray movingly makes clear that social change litigation is not really about law; it is about people.

– Chris Hansen, Esq. - Lead Counsel for Plaintiffs 1975;1973-1975 Mental Health Law Project;1975-1983 NYCLU;1983-1993 ACLU Children's Rights Project;1993-2012 ACLU National Legal

* * *

As a parent and lead Attorney in the Willowbrook case, Murray Schneps gives us a revealing inspirational account of the events leading up to the closing of the Willowbrook State School that housed 6000 children with intellectual disabilities, which represented the neglect and abuse that was perpetrated by a political system that was indifferent to the needs of the most fragile and vulnerable in our society.

"I SEE YOUR FACE BEFORE ME" is an account told with compelling clarity of the unconditional love a father had for his seriously disabled daughter, Lara, and his unwavering determination to develop a better life for her and the thousands of children with intellectual disabilities. Murray Schneps has demonstrated in his legal battles with the State of New York, that in providing alternative support for those with severe disabilities there can be no compromise. The closing of

Willowbrook was the beginning of a transformation to the supportive service and community inclusion that families, and those with disabilities, enjoy today.

This very detailed account of the Willowbrook Consent Decree and the eventual closing of Willowbrook on Staten Island remind us of the obligation we have to protect the civil rights of all of our citizens

– Don Rieb – Executive Director, Aid to the Developmentally Disabled, Riverhead, NY

* * *

I See Your Face Before Me is really a love story, a story of a father's love for his daughter and how that love led to his personal transformation and also inspired social and political change. In it we get a glimpse of a young lawyer with no particular interest in civil rights that grows to use his skills to advocate on behalf of those unable to speak for themselves. The Willowbrook story is not just about making sure that its residents were better cared for but about helping society in general to realize that basic human rights were being denied to a group of our fellow human beings and was morally wrong. For families with loved ones with developmental or mental disabilities, the book encourages them to become advocates even when they feel that they are not capable of such action. One person can make a difference and when others join in a common purpose the impossible becomes possible.

– Michael Mascari - Executive Director, Nassau County AHRC, Brookville, NY

I thought I knew the Willowbrook story until I read this book. It is an accurate historical record that reads like a novel.

– Walter Stockton – Chief Executive Officer, Independent Group Home Living Program, Inc. (IGHL), Manorville, NY

* * *

Murray Schneps has successfully captured the heart wrenching journey individuals with intellectual disabilities experienced during the Willowbrook years. As an architect of the Willowbrook Consent Decree, Murray engages us in the transformative process brought about by the closing of the Willowbrook State School, through the prism of his daughter Lara. It is an extraordinary tale that transcends the world of intellectual developmental disabilities and captures the heart of anyone who has faced a challenge. He weaves us through two decades of change thrust upon the New York State system with remarkable detail and unique insight. He shares with the reader his personal journey and how his daughter inspired him to altering a deeply fractured system.

– Peter Smergut - Executive Director, Life's WORC, Garden City, New York

* * *

I SEE YOUR FACE BEFORE ME is a unique, personal father's perspective of a time and a place that forever changed the world for children and adults with Developmental Disabilities. For everyone involved, it forever changed our lives as well. It is filled with personal anger and hope, tragedy and triumph

I did not agree with every opinion and view, but I agree that Murray Schneps is a pivotal figure and hero of this struggle. This is his story to tell. It is well worth reading and remembering

– Edward R. Matthews – Chief Executive Officer, United Cerebral Palsy of New York City, New York, NY

* * *

Murray Schneps has two stories to tell in I SEE YOUR FACE BEFORE ME: A FATHER'S PROMISE. The first is the story of a young couple embarking on their life together, crystalized and made sacred by the birth of their first child, a beautiful baby they named Lara.

Let's call it human error, terrible human error. Through a last-minute complication, Lara should have been born through caesarean section but at the hospital in Brooklyn that night in 1968, there was no doctor available to perform the surgery. As a result, over the months that followed, the effects of Lara's traumatic birth emerged, one after another: her blindness, her brain damage, her inability to meet one single developmental milestone, and, finally, the news that nothing, nothing, could be done to help Lara. The second story tells what really happened.

Grieving, numb, yet hopeful, Murray Schneps, a young attorney, and his then-wife set out to do their best for their child. They researched schools, institutions, having Lara live at home. Each possibility proved worse than the last. The turning point was perhaps the highly recommended Willowbrook, on Staten Island, where, they were told, Lara would be given every chance possible. Trusting, they sent Lara to Willowbrook but soon found that the conditions for inmates--if you will--of every age were beyond squalid, beyond Dickensian. This was no place for Lara, or for anyone. Nor was anyplace else they could find, anywhere. taking on the care and treatment of our society's weakest and most vulnerable became a legal quest for Schneps, and his "Father's Promise" is fulfilled as he recounts his--and others'--dedication to changing the hardest and harshest kind of system to change: one that has been put in place to deny even the need for such a system. There have been changes for the better made since Schneps made his promise to Lara, but the story doesn't end with her story or his or some legislation but perhaps not enough. This book is a story of a father's love, and an attorney's mission, a mission ongoing today. This call for compassion is timeless.

– Cheryl Merser – Author (Honorable Intentions; Grown-ups; A Starter Garden; Relax, It's Only Dinner; Cooking Tools; The Garden Design Book).

* * *

I SEE YOUR FACE BEFORE ME

A FATHER'S PROMISE

MURRAY B. SCHNEPS

A
MURRAY B. SCHNEPS
PUBLICATION

A
MURRAY B. SCHNEPS
PUBLICATION

ISBN: 978-0-9862489-0-0

Library of Congress – LCNN:

Printed in the United States of America

Cover design by Jason P. Mullins – based on a photo with
Lara and her father, Murray B. Schneps (circa 1974-5)

Interior design by Eli Blyden of Crunch Time Graphics

I SEE YOUR FACE BEFORE ME
Words by HOWARD DIETZ
Music by ARTHUR SCHWARTZ
© 1937 (Renewed) CHAPPELL & CO., INC. and
ARTHUR SCHWARTZ MUSIC
All Rights Reserved

I SEE YOUR FACE BEFORE ME, by Arthur Schwartz
and Howard Dietz
Used by permission

CONTENTS

PART ONE

PART TWO

PART THREE

ACKNOWLEDGEMENTS

I express my appreciation to Michael Simon, an editor, for his ideas and patience that moved my story forward.

With gratitude, love and appreciation to my darling wife, Teri Maurelli, who made it possible for this book to become a reality with her guidance, advice, editing, proof reading and reminding me of what I previously told her about my life. Without her assistance there would have been no book.

Thanks to my friend, Cheryl Merser, who guided me and believed in my story and to my son, Joshua Schneps, and friends/cohorts, Michael Lottman and Chris Hansen, who provided excellent thoughts, ideas and guidance.

I also must thank my children Elizabeth, Samantha and Joshua who involuntarily shared their parents commitment to help Lara, and finally, I thank and acknowledge my former wife, Vicki Schneps Yunis, who formed with me a unified irresistible force to help our Lara and developmentally disabled persons everywhere.

MALACHY'S FOREWORD

In the interest of full disclosure let me make it clear that the author of this book, Murray Schneps, is and has been my friend for over 40 years. It all began with Willowbrook. My wife Diana has a daughter Nina from her previous marriage who is severely autistic but that was no obstacle to Diana agreeing to marry me thus beginning a journey into areas we could never imagine but that is another story. This is the story of Murray Schneps who always planned on having a large family. Several years after he married Vicki their first child arrived in the person of their daughter, Lara, who was thoroughly and joyfully welcomed by her parents and their respective families. Before Lara's birth there was nary a cloud on the horizon. Not for one second does any parent want to acknowledge even the slightest deficiency in the little creature that has just entered their home and captured all the hearts therein. Sniffles perhaps a slight temperature at times perhaps but no more. However, in very short order the Schneps were torn from their domestic tranquility and flung into the maelstrom of what purported to be society's care for our children. Their frantic search for reassurance and services was met with a wall of denial, evasion, ignorance and deceit.

Then came the State of New York, which under Rockefeller had placed the problems of children with their various forms of intellectual and developmental disabilities in the hands of psychiatrists. That is akin to putting manual laborers in charge of the space program. Thousands of people with various handicaps, many of whom were greatly misdiagnosed, were thrown into the institutions. The largest was Willowbrook, formerly an army hospital built after World War II, which looked like something that had been designed by Josef Stalin. This cesspool of screaming, joyless, injured humanity was the destination for Lara, plus 5500 other citizens, including my stepdaughter, Nina.

Bland as it looked from the outside Willowbrook contained all the evils that big institutions cultivate as if they were attended by satanic minds paid to create the most horrendous conditions possible. Huge rooms devoid of furniture filled with skinny naked bodies of human beings lying in their own filth and excretions. The constant screams, shouts and moans emitting from suffering and disregarded miserable people seeking the ease from relentless pain and agony. How could we possibly put our children in such a hellhole? Before you get on your moral high horse I suggest you read this book to find out the reasons.

Moreover, this is a love story, Murray's love for Lara, and, like all love stories, it has its ups and downs, its defeats and triumphs. Even its failures led to further successes and, in spite of it all it is still a love story. Murray Schneps has told his story well and paid generous tribute to those who marched together in the conflict that wrought historic changes in the philosophy and the treatment of citizens who could not advocate for themselves. Robert Kennedy once visited Willowbrook and was shocked and appalled at what he witnessed but not even the Kennedy power and influence could change Willowbrook. So what did?

The war in Vietnam was tearing our country apart. The young people were waking up and getting wise to the rights granted by our Constitution. They were demanding the right to live and the end of stupid wars. At the time that Murray was pressuring the administrations of Willowbrook, the State of New York and the parent organization, inside the wards of Willowbrook compassionate staffs were demanding an end to institutional inhumanity. People like Dr. Michael Wilkins, social worker Elizabeth Lee, Dr. William Bronson and Ira Fisher risked their jobs by speaking out against the conditions at Willowbrook. Brilliant people like Bernard Carabello, who was grossly misdiagnosed, were subverting the system from inside. Angry parents began organizing, no longer cowed by threats of retribution to their loved ones. The New York Civil Liberties Union and the Legal Aid Society offered their services. Dr. Michael Wilkins persuaded Geraldo Rivera to bring his cameras in the back door to reveal the ongoing horrors of Willowbrook. It was a timely confluence of those with talent, skills, and commitment and the unbending person we all relied upon, Murray Schneps, as a leader against the ignorance of maintaining institutions for the developmentally disabled.

I am grateful to Murray Schneps for his courage and for never forgetting our goals, the development of a system of family style homes and the closing the institutions. He always insisted upon the delivery of appropriate services for all people in need. He set out to share his vision of what could be and he utilized the law, his passion, compassion, energy and remarkable tenacity to become the conscience and inspiration of the Willowbrook Review Panel and the parents' protector. I thank him for his brilliant legal mind, reminding us of the battles for justice and for enshrining that little warrior, Lara, who was an endless reminder of our goals to the leaders in this amazing revolution. If you do not shed a tear at the end of this book get your heart examined it may have stopped working!

– MALACHY McCOURT

I SEE YOUR FACE
BEFORE ME

A FATHER'S PROMISE

PROLOGUE

On December 26, 1937, in Brownsville, Brooklyn, New York, Sam Rubin Schneps and Hannah Kandel Schneps had their third child, a son, Murray Bernard Schneps. As young teenagers in the early 1920's, Sam and Hannah had emigrated from Poland to New York City. They were first cousins and had lived in nearby towns in Poland. When I was three years old we moved from Brownsville to the "fancy neighborhood" of Brighton Beach, also Brooklyn. My mother cautioned me not to curse or fight or to be loud or noisy. But I insisted that this was not really such a fancy place, the kids here said "f--k and s--t and hit and screamed, too."

My father was an honorable man and an ethical kosher butcher. He ultimately owned his own butcher store and, of course, never used his thumb on the scale to ramp up the price. He did not have the opportunity to attend school much beyond his Bar Mitzvah at age 13 but he was bright and capable and could calculate a column of numbers with the alacrity and accuracy of a modern computer. My father did not believe in showing affection to his children and ascribed to the school of hard knocks "git arein in tuches, gait arein in kupf," if information is given in the rear end it will enter the head. But he was mostly a kind and compassionate man. I loved and admired him. I appreciated who and what he was and had accomplished, though there was a learning curve.

My mother was a beautiful and amazing woman and a nurturing mother. She was sweet and knew how to get along with everyone. She was a private person and hated loud talking or yelling. "Sha shtill," be still, she would insist. However, she was not against speaking up when confronted with rude or unfair behavior. She just preferred to use her intellect surgically, rather than resort to a noisy confrontation. My mother could be found in the butcher store working as a cashier, during busy days and prior to the Jewish holidays, or square dancing at the Brighton Beach Baths.

My grandfather, my Zayda, was a very orthodox Jewish man. Remarkably, he was an extraordinary wise and liberal man. He was not the kind of Zayda who hugged and kissed you or was your buddy; rather, he was eminent and religious. To me, he spoke directly with G-d[1]. I respected him tremendously. I could never be one so eminent.

My grandmother, my Bubba, died when I was about eight. I remember her as the typical immigrant grandma, wonderful smells coming from her kitchen, warm and noisy family celebrations at her table, and her love and pride swirling around us.

I do not think my parents quite understood or approved of my athletic activities and pursuits. Perhaps it was not what a nice Jewish boy was supposed to want but I was very active and a pretty good athlete. I was lean and wirey and I learned early, as many urban boys did, that appearing meek or easily bullied would make my life more difficult.

---

[1] My Zayda taught me that the name in the Lord may not be used in vain so G-d was spelled by omitting the "0" and replacing the letter with a dash.

Luckily, despite my lack of bulk, I possessed a strong and a powerful engine, physically and mentally. I enjoyed wrestling and boxing but never started a fight. However, I did enjoy finishing one. My chosen defense was a half nelson or a crushing headlock.

I attended Elementary School P.S. 225, Abraham Lincoln High School and graduated from Brooklyn College. My parents liked me and were very proud of me. After all, I was the first of my family to graduate from college and then from graduate school. It was a big deal. At my graduation from Brooklyn Law School, my father stood, raised his arms and cheered for me. Even though I was embarrassed back in 1961, I later learned to cherish the scene.

I married Pearl Vicki Adler on August 3, 1963, she became Vicki Schneps and our story unfolded. Since it began 50 years ago, my memory is not precise. Much of the personal conversations are compilations, true and fair representations of what was said and occurred, to the best of my recollection. The conversations are supported by the original records of the Willowbrook Review Panel held by the State University at Albany, the Willowbrook Class Action and the Suffolk Developmental Class Action located at the National Archives, the New York Times and the Staten Island Advance articles and photographs preserved on the company web sites, personal records and photographs, and indelible memories burned in my mind. The depositions and courtroom dialogues are repeated verbatim from the records.

PART ONE

1

A NEW LIFE

Vicki packed her nightgowns, her toiletries and her extra toothbrush into an overnight bag. She had prepared for this day weeks in advance. She was ready to begin a new life and so was I.

"The doctor said we should arrive at the hospital after midnight," she said. "That way, we'll save the cost of an extra day."

"Imagine that, a frugal doctor."

"You don't like Dr. Wilen." Vicki faced me at the door and I took the overnight bag. It was 1968, she was 24, nine months pregnant, and beautiful. I was 31, a rising lawyer, and my life was bursting with possibility.

"You're happy with Dr. Wilen, so she's fine with me," I said.

Vicki smiled, kissed me, and waddled out the door with as much grace as was possible.

She was in the early stages of labor, with contractions coming thirty minutes apart. To kill time until midnight, we went to see a movie about a family with twelve children,

"Cheaper by the Dozen." We giggled throughout the film. Twelve children seemed excessive but I always wanted six. I could hardly wait to hold my first, my prince or my princess, a gift to the world.

"Did you figure out what to say in the announcement cards?" she asked on the way to Brooklyn Jewish Hospital.

"I will."

But I already knew what I was going to write. Until the birth, it was my secret. "And now we are three. My Darling, my Darling's Darling and, humbly, me." I would add the details underneath.

By the time we got to the hospital it was May 23rd, labor was progressing with contractions coming five minutes apart. The admission lady directed Vicki to a private labor room and changed her into a white hospital gown. She pouted at being forced into such unflattering attire. I said, "I promise, after the baby comes, we'll find something prettier." The room was barely six-by-nine, the walls were light gray, and the furnishings limited to a hospital bed and a bottle of saline solution hanging from a pole connected to Vicki's arm. We smiled nervously at each other. Here was the beginning of our journey to parenthood. No turning back now. Oh, boy!

When the doctor came in to see Vicki they parked me in a waiting room. The waiting room was a sparsely furnished cube, with the same light gray walls, a pole lamp and a brown naugahyde sofa. It felt like a hip, modern jail cell.

I waited and waited. After four or five hours the doctor came to see me. "She's having strong contractions," the doctor said. "She's lost some blood but we haven't made a lot of progress toward delivery."

"What does that mean?"

"Just that. I'll keep you posted."

Four more hours with no company except the second hand going around the clock at a snail's pace. The doctor came out to tell me more of nothing. She lost blood. No progress. I could not help but notice all the blood on the doctor's gown.

This time I spoke up. "Listen, Dr. Wilen, I'm a sophisticated and knowledgeable person. If she needs a cesarean section, do it! I have no prejudice against a cesarean."

"It's not time yet. We'll see."

I fished out some change from my pocket and headed to the phone booth. The sun had come up. The morning shift entered the hospital, and our journey continued.

In spite of Dr. Wilen's assurances, I believed that things were not going well. In fact, I was fearful and did not want to be alone. I dialed my brother Herbie.

He was the middle child of three children. My sister, Millie, was the oldest. I was the baby. Herbie and I had been on bad terms for years, maybe always. He answered on the fourth ring.

"Hello?"

"Herbie, it's Murray."

"Yeah?"

Not surprisingly, there was no warmth in his greeting. It made my request even harder.

I said, "Vicki's in labor and it's not going well. It's bad. Real bad. Can you get down here? I need you. We're at Brooklyn Jewish Hospital."

He said, "Okay, Murray. I'm leaving right now!" Which says something about brothers. Or at least about *my* brother.

It must have been around 1:00 p.m. when Herbie arrived, shook my hand, put his arm around my shoulder, gave me a cup of coffee and sat with me. I told him what he had missed. Dr. Wilen came out again.

"The baby's head isn't turning. It appears to be a brow presentation."

"What does that mean?"

"We need to perform a cesarean section."

Great idea. If only I had suggested it seven hours ago.

"Are you doing it right now?"

"Oh, not right now, I have to bring in a surgeon."

"Why?"

"I'm not qualified to perform a cesarean."

She turned on her heel and vanished.

Dr. Wilen did not perform a cesarean section hours ago, when she should have, because she was not qualified to perform surgery or was unable to recognize the need.

At least now the baby would be born. Vicki had had a rough night and a rough day, but the worst was behind us.

At about 4:00 P.M., a surgeon I had never met before came out of the delivery room holding my bundle of joy. "Mr. Schneps?"

I had been awake for two days, but I knew my name.

"Congratulations! It's a girl!" The surgeon pulled down the blanket to prove the point, but what I saw seemed to appear the opposite.

"What are you talking about? That's a boy!" I was about to start yelling at him.

"Sir. That's the umbilical cord."

"Oh." He lifted it. "Oh. Okay." Boy, was I embarrassed.

She did not cry but layed peacefully and comfortably in the doctor's arms, and then in mine. "She's beautiful," I said. "An angel." The top of her head was covered with orange fuzz like a perfect peach, accented by a red spot at the peak of her forehead. I relaxed and all seemed fine.

Herbie laid a hand on my shoulder. "You did good, Moish."

Moish. Nobody called me that anymore. It felt good.

"Does she have a name?"

We had gone over this. If it was a boy, Joshua. And a girl?

"Lara," I said. "Lara Rebecca." I tried it out. "Hi, Lara. Hi, baby. Daddy loves you."

Vicki chose the name from a character in the movie, "Dr. Zivago."

It must have been 7:00 P.M., a few hours after the delivery, when Vicki's parents arrived. I marched them down the hall from the waiting room to the nursery to show off my baby.

"How will we know it's her?" someone asked.

"Because she's the most beautiful baby in the world, is how. And the sign reading 'Schneps' on the bassinet."

As we got to the window, I noticed that one of the babies had turned blue. All blue. Face, hands-the works. My mother-in-law went nuts.

"My God! The baby! Look!"

I could not see the child clearly. I could not tell if it was Lara. I was frantically looking to read the name on the bassinet but my eyes went blurry. I started blinking, trying to focus, and in a flash the nurses closed the blinds, covering the window.

Vicki's mother started to scream. "It's Lara! The baby! It's Lara!"

I turned to her. "Shut up!" I shouted. "Just shut up! It's not Lara! It's not!"

She clapped her hand over her mouth and looked up at me with tears in her eyes. There were twenty babies in that nursery. There was no reason to think the blue one was Lara. But both of us believed the worst. And for a moment both of us believed that what we said made a difference.

A short time later I knew she was right. The blue baby was Lara. But I did not need a hysterical mother-in-law at that moment. What's more, it was *my* crisis, not hers. I thought it was indelicate of her to out-mourn the mourner.

The next thing I remember was me standing in the hallway with the Chief Pediatric Resident, David Levy, M.D.

"Lara's fine. She was blue for a short period of time."

"How short?"

"We don't know exactly."

"See, that's the thing. She was really blue. I didn't realize it was her. And to me it seemed like a long period of time."

He seemed rattled for a moment but he put on his calm face again. "I wouldn't worry."

Lara went home in a timely way and we moved her into her beautiful bedroom, lovingly decorated with reddish furniture. The room was large and sunny with a window looking out over the Cross Island Parkway and Little Neck Bay, and the apartment complex swimming pool.

She was so sweet and so beautiful. She was a week old and she was mine. The red mark on her forehead disappeared. Her orange hair was even more pronounced and was contrasted by her creamy skin and blue-gray eyes. Her face lit up my life.

My mother, a petite and beautiful woman, came to fuss over Lara at the first chance. She sat on the sofa feeding Lara her bottle, a diaper draped over her floral print dress. Vicki was getting a well-earned nap.

"Mom, did you notice her head and her body are in perfect proportion?"

"Of course they are! Because she's perfect! Perfect!"

I was still trying to get Mom to consider the head-size issue. "No, I mean…aren't babies supposed to have big heads? In relation to their bodies?"

She stared me down. "You're looking for something to worry about."

"Really?"

"All my babies had small heads. And look at you! So smart, a lawyer. You're worrying over nothing."

"Oh," I said. "Okay."

Mom turned to Lara. "But baby!" she said. "Why so long with the bottle?"

It was true, no matter who fed her, Lara had trouble sucking from the bottle. A bottle of formula took her forever to drink. And at eight weeks old, Dr. Spock was clear that she should be able to meet our gaze. But that never happened for Lara. Her eyes met ours but fleetingly and, it appeared, by chance.

Then we noticed Lara's face would freeze as if she were yawning. I thought she was getting sleepy. As the "yawns" continued, she began holding the position for longer periods. We did not think this was normal but really had no idea what we were witnessing. We were scared. What was going on?

The pediatrician said she was having petit mal seizures, and referred Lara to Richard Reuben, M.D., a pediatric neurologist. In early September 1968 Lara was hospitalized at Long Island Jewish for various tests, including an electroencephalogram (EEG). We went to his office for the results, Vicki cradling Lara.

"The tests are inconclusive."

Vicki and I looked at each other, then at him. I said, "inconclusive?"

"She's too young to rely on such results."

I had a lot of questions but I could not put them into words.

He said, "the results do not conclusively indicate epilepsy or other seizure disorders. However, the results do not indicate that she does *not* have these conditions. They are simply inconclusive. Lara's brain is too young and immature for us to be able to draw definitive conclusions."

"Is that it, Dr. Reuben?," I said. I was not happy without a conclusive result. I needed to know the truth. I was able to deal with any truth, develop a plan and attack the problem. But not knowing was intolerable.

When we returned to our pediatrician, he was less than reassuring or supportive. "We don't always explain all the details to nervous mothers like you. But if you like, I can prescribe something."

Vicki asked, "For the seizures?"

"For your nerves."

Vicki stormed out to the car.

"What kind of way is that to talk to a new mother?"

"No kind of way."

"And what if I *am* nervous. Who wouldn't be?"

I unlocked the car.

Vicki got in and held Lara in her arms.

I said, "*I'd* be nervous. I *am* nervous."

"You're nervous. And you're a lawyer."

I did not know what that meant but I did not see a reason to argue. We settled into the front seat and closed the door. I did not start the engine.

"What?" she said.

"Maybe there's something else."

"What do you mean?"

"I keep thinking."

I did not say this part out loud. Dr. Wilen did not do the cesarean when she should have. Not because it was not time but because she was unqualified to perform a cesarean. We lived in a world where people believed in doctors. It was hard to believe that doctors had limitations.

I continued, "They keep saying things like inconclusive, nervous, too young to tell. Things that don't mean anything."

"So?"

"Maybe they *know* the truth but they can't tell us. Maybe they don't know how."

A few months later when we were feeding Lara, her head suddenly jerked forward and down, her mouth opened wide, her arms shot out to the sides, and she doubled over as though struck. We thought she was startled but there was no obvious reason for her reaction. Perhaps she had a hiccup, we speculated.

At first the motions came intermittently but by the next day they occurred simultaneously and repeated more and more frequently, hour after hour. Each occurrence seemed to make her more and more lethargic. She did not cry or act as if she was in any pain. She only got more and more flaccid. Feeding her, already a challenge, became an art form. Getting food into her between each episode required remarkable timing and persistence.

We got her back to Dr. Reuben and learned that she had developed myoclonic (salaam) seizures. The seizures were persistent and unrelenting. She had hundreds of them every hour.

Lara was again hospitalized in hopes of stopping the seizures. Based upon her most recent EEG, Dr. Reuben reported that Lara's brain showed a pattern called "hypsarrythmia." While that seemed informative to him, I had no idea what he was talking about. I could not even form an intelligent question about what that meant for my daughter.

I went to the library at the New York Academy of Medicine, in uptown Manhattan, and studied textbooks regarding brain damage, microcephaly and myoclonic seizures. Microcephaly means an abnormally small head. Soon, I was better able to understand what the doctors were telling us and to ask better questions.

I learned that hypsarrythmia was random high-voltage slow brain waves and spikes observed in infants. It is characterized by jackknife seizures that are commonly associated with mental retardation. "It's imperative to control and stop the seizures. The longer the seizures persist, the worse her prognosis," Dr. Reuben told me.

They gave her phenobarbital, Dilantin, ACTH and, ultimately, large doses of prednisone. The prednisone caused her to absorb water, so her face, neck and shoulders swelled greatly. Her head became very heavy. She awoke every two hours needing to drink. Her diaper was constantly sopping wet and sleeping at night was intermittent, at best. Lara would cry for hours. The only relief for her, and for me, was when I held her and walked with her. She loved to be held in my arms. She would nestle into my shoulder and I could feel her tiny body relax. It felt so good to hold her. I held her and walked with her and sang to her for hours. It was the one plus, this Daddy and Lara time. I would sing many songs, lots of lullabies. But most often it was my favorite, a Sinatra tune. I liked crooning and Lara was my best audience:

I see your face before me
Crowding my every dream...

Knowing that the myoclonic seizures were the enemy, every effort was made to eliminate them. The administration of large doses of prednisone slowed the frequency and intensity of the seizures and soon thereafter they were completely controlled. While that brought her great relief, the termination of the seizures did not result in any real improvement in Lara. She remained the same unresponsive child, only without myoclonic seizures. A day for celebration was not in the cards. Dr. Reuben had nothing else to offer us in terms of advice or other procedures. Lara did not improve. It was time for us to secure another opinion.

"I want to get a second opinion," I said.

"This is a perfect time for you to do so," he replied.

"Who would you recommend," I asked?

Dr. Reuben recommended a pediatric neurologist at Columbia Presbyterian Hospital in Manhattan. However, from my research I already knew of the Chief of Pediatric Neurology at Columbia Presbyterian Hospital, Dr. Arnold Gold.

"Thank you Dr. Reuben. We will see both the physician you recommend and also Dr. Gold. I have heard about him and feel that I need to see him as well."

"I know Dr. Gold and he is a wonderful physician. If you see Dr. Gold you don't need to see anyone else."

"If you feel that I should see the other doctor you suggested, I can see both of them."

"No, it is not necessary for you to consult with both of them. Dr. Gold is the Chief and he has great and extensive experience and knowledge. I can arrange for an appointment with him."

Dr. Reuben arranged for an early appointment for us to visit Dr. Gold, in spite of the fact that he was very busy. Without Dr. Reuben's interceding for us, an early appointment would not have been available. Dr. Gold agreed to see us during his lunch hour, a time he jealously protected.

Lara's face got so bloated that when Dr. Gold examined her he did not realize that she had a definite bridge on her nose. She did. She was very beautiful but it was not possible for him to see that she had a bridge on her nose. I never noticed that her bridge seemed to have disappeared. Her cheeks, head, neck and upper back were so puffed up with retained water from the prednisone, that her little nose seemed to have been swallowed by her cheeks. Some people may have thought that her appearance was grotesque but she was *my* beautiful little girl. I saw nothing but my Lara, my beautiful Lara.

Dr. Gold sat us down. We were sitting in a large private office with three walls lined with wooden shelves covered with medical books. The fourth wall had a large window, his framed degrees, a painting and a huge wooden desk. Dr. Gold sat in a high backed swivel chair upholstered in dark green leather. We sat, sinking in a matching leather couch, and awaited his verdict.

"First of all," he said.

As he spoke I looked at her nose, wondering how something so tiny could have such consequence. And I looked back at Dr. Gold. He was not hiding his face in a file. He was not telling Vicki she was a nervous mother. He was nervous. I liked him. I just did not like what he was saying. He went on.

"She is…micro cephalic. Do you know what that means?"

I knew that one. "She has a small head."

He nodded. "And she has a very high palate. All of which indicated that Lara…"

He paused to wipe the sweat from his lip. And I noticed that he referred to Lara by her name. "All indicators are that Lara will be profoundly mentally retarded."

The long labor, the oxygen loss in the nursery, the seizures; everything, it seemed, was either a cause or an effect. Vicki looked up at me and choked back a sob. I was stunned. I felt as if I had been kicked in the stomach. But I was not a stranger to pain, I was a product of the streets of Brooklyn.

Back in the mid 1940s Victor Blum lived down the block from me on Brighton 12th Street in Brighton Beach. I was about eight years old when Victor and I got into an argument and began to shove each other. Victor was two years older than me and a head taller. Suddenly, he bent down, grabbed my testicles and squeezed. He would not let go. So I grabbed his head in a headlock and squeezed his head with my arms. It did not matter how much pain I was in. I knew I would not stop squeezing his head until he let go of me. I would never give up, he would have to stop first. And he did and then I did. I always knew that I could hold on as long as I had to.

There are some things I cannot do. But I *can* hold on, as long as I need to.

From the moment I witnessed newborn Lara turning blue at Brooklyn Jewish Hospital, I was already concerned that she might be brain damaged. The labor lasted too long. She had been blue for a long time, which meant a long time without oxygen. Dr. Levy assured me that she was all right but I never truly felt reassured. Every day I spent with Lara, I became more suspicious. She was a beautiful baby, no question about it. Her orange hair, perfect features and creamy skin - all perfect. But much as it pained me to think it, she was *not* normal. She was not like other babies. She still had trouble with her bottle. She never made eye contact with me or anyone else. She seemed to become less and less, rather than more and more. She could not sit up, roll over or hold up her own head.

And when she began having seizures, my beliefs were confirmed. "Well, so what?" I thought. "She won't be brilliant. I can handle that." I had always been lucky. I was a tough kid from Brooklyn, lucky enough to have the right teachers who encouraged me to stay in school and put my shoulder to the wheel. I went to college, played college baseball and then went to law school. Things always fell into place. I was a lucky guy and would continue to be lucky.

I tried to negotiate with G-d but some deals cannot be made no matter how smart or tough you are. I did not lose often but I thought I might lose this one.

Each new day, week and month, each new illness, made it more clear that my Lara would never have a life of independence. I knew that G-d did not accept my bargain. I stood on the balcony late one night staring at the stars and thinking, "What have I done? What have I done to deserve this? Whatever it is, *punish ME!*" I prayed. I ranted at G-d. But I did not cry. I felt that I had to be strong, stronger than Victor Blum or anyone who ever threw anything at me.

Keep squeezing, Victor Blum! You will give up before I do.

This pain was far worse than anything I had previously experienced and it would never go away, even if someone stopped squeezing.

Dr. Gold believed Lara was profoundly retarded and that she would be profoundly retarded forever. Vicki sobbed quietly. I was stunned. I felt like I was doubled over. We had been dealt a terrible blow.

As we drove home from Dr. Gold's office along the Cross Island Parkway, a light flashed in the rear view mirror.

"Pull over," Vicki said.

"What?"

"Pull over. The police want you."

"Did I do something wrong?"

I managed to pull over. The cop surveyed us, a young, distraught couple with a baby.

"Sir, you know you were speeding?"

"No," I said, dazed. "I didn't know."

"Where are you coming from?"

"The doctor."

"Were you sedated?"

I tried to remember what had happened at the doctor's office.

"He told us our daughter is profoundly retarded."

There was a silence. Finally he said, "Sir, I have children of my own, and I understand. Would you do me a favor?"

"Sure."

"Would you get yourself together and be sure to protect your wife, your child, and other citizens by driving carefully?"

He did not give me a ticket.

2

THE QUEST BEGINS

When Dr. Gold gave us the bad news about Lara, he was as kind as he could have been. But it was his job to give us the whole, unwashed, direct truth. He did that without sugarcoating or evading the truth. That blunt assessment stunned us. But we knew that a real plan was required. I was a scrapper, a fighter. I would figure it out. And Vicki was always a "cockeyed optimist." She would keep us from getting discouraged.

I stood over Lara in her crib, thinking as she slept. As a lawyer, I could work hard and make enough money to take care of her and protect her. But I knew I would not be around forever, so my plans had to project her beyond my lifetime. Trust fund? Long term care? Therapy? Other services? "I will always protect you sweet girl. I promise!"

Short-term care was tough enough. Our first goal was to find an aide or assistant to help us at home.

"We have money coming in," Vicki said. "What's this like for people who can't even afford help?"

"We have to find a program," I said.

"Something to help her develop to her greatest potential," she added.

I was working long days like any young lawyer. I would get home at 7:00 or 8:00 p.m. on a good night, ride the elevator up, then run from the elevator to the apartment to see Lara as soon as possible. I needed to be with her, sit with her, hold her. But I felt compelled to assess her improvements. I was searching for some sign of change. Any change, no matter how tiny, would make my world. It was as if they had said she would never grow and I kept running home to measure her height. Each day I came home hopeful but, alas, each day I was disappointed. We tried everything we could think of. We hung multiple mobiles above her crib. An array of dancing, jiggling, jumping, clicking, singing, soothing and loud toys failed to attract Lara's attention. Nothing worked. She actually lost ground. Initially, she could hold her head up. Now, sometimes it would flop over when not supported. Even with her ever-increasing general spasticity, her head became increasingly more floppy.

I constructed a blinking light and placed it over her crib to capture her wandering gaze. We explained this to one of her many doctors.

The doctor sat behind his oak desk, making notes in Lara's file. Sun streamed through the window. Lara was cradled on Vicki's lap, quietly. The smile never left Vicki's face, her badge of relentless optimism, but I could discern the fear in her eyes as she spoke.

"She never seems to focus," Vicki said. "She looks everywhere but never focuses."

"She's blind," the doctor said. As if he were saying, "She's tired."

I seemed to lose my balance but I was still upright. I looked to Vicki. The shadow of a smile hung onto her face. "What?" she asked.

The doctor looked up from his file, squinted at us as if he could not decide whether we were processing the information. "I thought you knew."

I thought you knew.

It turned out, the doctors were not sure whether her blindness was due to injuries to her optic nerves or due to brain injury that prevented her from perceiving sight. Did her eyes fail to function or did her brain fail to perceive? No one knew that answer.

Either way, she was blind. Profoundly retarded, and blind. As if being profoundly retarded was not hard enough. As if she was not missing enough of life. Now she would not even see it, not a sunset, not a flower, not her daddy's smile.

"If this is part of G-d's plan," I thought, "I can think of a better plan."

To make things worse, her ability to hold her head up grew less each day. She could not sit alone, or roll over, or make any repetitive sounds except something like "ah din," uttered when she appeared to be happy. We fed her by holding her in our arms to support her body and head. And, always, we snuggled and kissed her and continued to speak and sing to her. If she could only respond.

But she could laugh, how she could laugh. Hysterically, sometimes. Odd sounds set her off. She liked the sound of coughing, the louder and rougher, the better. If I was drinking water and some went down the wrong way, my coughing set her off. She howled. When I got my breath back, I said, "We should send her on vacation to a TB ward. She'll laugh all day."

When she reached four months of age, we started looking for an appropriate school for her. If there was such a school, we could not find it. The Department of Mental Hygiene was no help. They told us there were no day programs and that Lara should be institutionalized.

Vicki called me at work and read me the brochures.

"There's a day program in the Bronx, created and operated by Dr. Jack…I think it's pronounced Gootzeit? Of the Institutes of Applied Human Dynamics."

I had to give 100% of my attention to the various civil cases I was handling that I was working on—I needed to work to support my family—but my family needed 100% too. So I gave 200%.

"Applied Human Dynamics. Keep reading."

"Parents attend with their children from 8:00 AM to 9:00 PM each day. It's a continuous day and night program that keeps the children moving their arms and legs and heads and bodies with exercises. If the child can't move, the parents move the body parts for them." It sounded like the "patterning" theory that later proved to be ineffective.

In "patterning," involuntary movements that were forced by others, would allegedly train the brain to learn the movements. The movements were performed all day with many teams of volunteers.

"Each day?"

"I guess I could go myself," Vicki said, sadly.

"Well, great. I'll see you next spring."

"It says that continuous activity is the answer for development."

We visited Dr. Jack Gootzeit at his Institute. Many parents and children of all ages were there in constant motion. Dr. Gootzeit examined Lara on a mat and vigorously pushed and pulled her arms and legs and head and trunk. He was a very large man and I was afraid he would hurt Lara. Of course, he did not.

On the way home I thought about what we had seen.

"Honey," I said, "this program is not right for our Lara or for us. I haven't discovered any success stories with this patterning theory."

"What, then?"

"Let's keep looking. I'll try anything that makes sense."

It was Lara's first winter. She was seven months old. We had a huge snowstorm. Four inches of snow on the ground, and traffic was impossible. Lara got sick. Her fever spiked to 103 degrees and she was having trouble breathing. Her nose was so tiny and her cold symptoms made her gasp and cry at the same time. We called our pediatricians to examine Lara. Even though they had previously made house calls to treat Lara, on this occasion they refused to come to us or to even give us an appointment at their offices. They essentially fired us. We felt abandoned.

We telephoned Dr. Reuben, our pediatric neurologist.

"Call Dr. Berman," he said.

"Who?"

"David Berman, his office is in Bayside, not far from your home."

He gave us the number. We dialed. "Dr. Reuben gave us your number. Our daughter Lara is sick, she has a 103 fever and is having breathing problems." An hour later, in the thick of the snowstorm, he knocked on our front door.

He renewed my faith in the medical profession. It was a good thing, too. I would need it.

When she was better we continued the search. We drove out to a private residential facility in an old house in Glen Cove, Long Island. It looked run-down on the outside but we tried to keep our spirits up.

The inside was no better. Profoundly retarded children and adults were strapped into feeding chairs. The chief activities seemed to be sitting, drooling and staring. A heavyset attendant in a soiled white uniform was watching TV.

"Excuse me," I said. She took her time turning away from the TV screen. This made me wonder how quickly she would respond to a child's need for help, especially someone who could not utter the word, "help."

"What."

"Who's in charge here?"

"You're looking at her."

"I mean, who's in charge of the program and training, the . . . services, for the residents?"

She looked at me like I had come from another planet and made no response. For the first time I realized what I was up against.

We visited more private facilities, all housed in small buildings or large old homes. All, like that first one, were not "habilitation facilities" and made no attempt at education or life training or skill development. They housed the children, more or less comfortably, until they died. "More or less" anything was not acceptable for my baby. They were more like "waiting rooms" for the Great Beyond.

Lara was profoundly retarded, blind, suffering some kind of physical disability I did not understand, and subject to random illnesses and seizures. I was a fighter and Vicki was an eternal optimist, but we were ready to hear some *good* news for a change.

We were hopeful that we would have some.

3

WILLOWBROOK

Designed in 1938 as a home for mentally retarded individuals and located in the Willowbrook section of Staten Island, the newly completed facility was first opened as a U.S. Army Hospital in 1942. After the war, in late 1947, the New York State Department of Mental Hygiene reopened the facility it had planned, calling it Willowbrook State School. Here, instead of just being locked up and out of sight, mentally retarded children were promised treatment and education, a real life. Here was the hope of progress.

On a bright, sunny Saturday, we climbed into our Buick Electra, drove through Queens around the perimeter of Brooklyn, across the Verrazano-Narrows Bridge and out to the Willowbrook campus. A guide pointed out a brand new complex of five so-called "baby buildings" in a circular layout with a large building, the children's therapy center, in the middle. Corridors led from the therapy center to connect to each residential building like spokes on a wheel. The children and staff would not have to battle rain, snow or cold. Each of the five residential buildings had four wards and each ward held fifty babies, totaling two hundred babies per building. A thousand babies.

It seemed like a lot.

The baby buildings we visited looked quite new. They were clean, well kept, brightly lit. Each ward was staffed with several direct care employees, called Mental Health Therapy Aids, MHTAs, or attendants. Best of all, the therapy building offered various types of therapy for Lara, including physical therapy, occupational therapy and speech therapy. Everything she would need. What was absent were personal possessions like, photographs, dolls, toys, pictures and the like. But we could easily supply that. We thought we had found heaven.

We decided to pursue Lara's admission.

But there was a long waiting list. "If you consider 12 to 24 months 'long.' Once she reaches the age of six, the wait goes up to six years, but at that point, forget it."

"We can offer you immediate admission," one helpful administrator said, "if you move her into the rubella unit."

Vicki and I looked at each other in horror.

"She doesn't have rubella," I said.

Vicki added hopefully, "she has other things!"

It turned out Willowbrook was involved in experimental research conducted by Dr. Saul Krugman of New York University Hospital, infecting the mentally retarded residents with rubella and hepatitis. Krugman's research was spurred by outbreaks of hepatitis at the school through the 1940s and 50s, making it an ideal testing ground.

"Thanks," I said, "she has enough problems without adding rubella."

Over the next two months we moved mountains to get her pushed up on the admissions list. We gathered her medical records and reports. We begged her doctors to write letters making Lara's condition seem even worse than it was, as if the reality was not bad enough. At one year of age Lara was not only blind and profoundly retarded, but she could not hold her head up or adequately suck liquid from a bottle and was subject to breathing problems. Because of her weak sucking, she could aspirate milk into her lungs. And still, we had to exaggerate her disabilities to get her admitted. We also asked the doctors to indicate that admission was vital for the physical and mental health of Lara *and of her parents*, who were planning to have more children.

It seemed so important for us to get her into this one school that would solve her problems, and ours. Such a solution, this heavenly named oasis: *"Willowbrook, a facility located in the midst of 375 acres of park land."* Get her into Willowbrook, we thought, even if it takes a word from the governor. Get her into Willowbrook, and everything will be fine.

The letter came. "Dear Mr. and Mrs. Schneps: We are pleased to inform you that your daughter Lara has been admitted..."

We hugged and danced in the kitchen. The campaign worked!

"What else does it say?"

"We're supposed to visit and meet with a social worker."

We marked the day and time on the calendar and smiled at each other, tears in our eyes. And we kissed. It was the happiest we had been since...

We were very happy.

The Administration Building, a large multi-storied brick structure, housed its main entrance on the second floor. You entered by climbing up one of the two open outside staircases that rose to large double doors on top of an inverted "V." We climbed up the left stairs. Outside the doors stood a short, round and balding man with a broad shining smile. He wore a wrinkled plaid flannel shirt, mismatched pants and a knit cap. He had the sweet, open demeanor common to those with Down syndrome.

He said, "Hi."

We ran in terror. We had climbed the stairs side by side, hand in hand. But now we divided, every man for himself, and went down separate staircases. We found each other, hugged, made it to a bench and caught our breath.

"What's the matter with us?"

"I don't know, I don't know."

What was the matter with us? He had spoken with the warmth of a child. Little that I know how lucky we would be if our Lara could do what he had done—look a stranger in the eye and say "hi!"

We were ignorant, naïve, afraid. We were like the rest of the world. But we had to get educated, and fast.

We climbed the stairs again.

The little man who had greeted us had many traits we would have wanted in a social worker. Warmth. Caring.

Eye contact. The social worker's desk was piled with papers. She had a half eaten sandwich and a bottle of Yoo-hoo from which she took swigs throughout our visit.

"How old is Laura."

"Lara. Thirteen months."

"What?"

"Lara. L. A. R. A."

"It says Laura!" she barked

"We're pretty sure it's Lara."

"Lara, Laura, what's the difference." She kept filling out boxes on the form. I opened my mouth to tell her exactly who did care, but Vicki laid a hand on my arm, as if to say: not now, choose your battles.

She showed us the ward.

Lara would live in a ward, not a bedroom like the one she had at home, her own room with her own dolls and carpet to crawl on and familiar smells and sounds. But a ward with hard terrazzo floors and the smell of disinfectant and beds, 50 of them stood end to end with raised sides to keep the kids from getting out on their own, and nurses and attendants. But we had considered all the options and this was the best one: residential but with training, education, habilitation, and not too far away to visit. All the boxes checked off in my brain but my guts twisted. So what? I am a smart man. Why listen to my guts? We did the research and took the action. Think of all the letters we wrote to get her into this place. We could not turn back now. Could we? Wasn't this what we wanted?

We delivered Lara to Willowbrook on July 31, 1969. It was a Thursday. We dropped her off with her bottles, a box of diapers, 14 pairs of pajamas, 6 dresses, 5 pairs of pants, 8 shirts, 6 tee shirts, 16 pairs of socks and 4 hats. We settled her in with the nurses in the ward. We hugged her and kissed her and told her we would be back soon.

We lied. We were not allowed to visit her for 30 days.

"It is in Lara's best interests," they said. My stomach kept turning over. Vicki kept a bright smile as tears rolled down her cheeks.

"Take care of our little girl," I said.

"We will," the nurse answered.

How could we explain to Lara that we were leaving? That we were leaving her somewhere away from home, with strangers? She would not even see us walk away.

We turned and walked out of the ward, down the hall and out to the parking lot.

Something happened in the pit of my stomach, as if I took a powerful punch. I almost doubled over. But I fought the urge. Vicki gripped my arm. Men don't cry, I thought. Not real men. Certainly not men from Brooklyn. And this was no time to be weak. This was a time to be strong. Only strength would win the day.

There was no going right back to the house without Lara in it. We knew that ahead of time. So we had made plans to go away for a few days to Ridgefield, Connecticut to meet friends who were on their honeymoon. Coincidently, our anniversary was August 3rd, that Sunday. The weekend would be a celebration.

At least we could pretend. We drove straight from Willowbrook, 2½ hours, to Connecticut, with nothing to break the agonizing silence except Vicki occasionally reading directions from the Triple-A map or choking back a sob and me just choking.

We settled into the unfamiliar bed that night with our vague hopes, our lack of alternatives, and the creeping sense that perhaps we had made a mistake.

The terrazzo floors, gray walls and end-to-end cribs gave Lara's ward a dark, tomb-like feel. But Lara brightened it up. If you paid attention to her, held her, touched her, or sang to her, she would smile and she would seem to communicate on some level. Even the most jaded, hardened adult likes to have that kind of effect on a child and she quickly became a favorite in the ward and Building 14. They placed her crib at the entry to the ward so she would always be in view of the staff and any visitors. The staff loved her and kept her clean and seemingly happy. I never saw a diaper rash while she was living in Willowbrook. I used this as a standard: diaper rash is a risk in big hospitals. The longer a baby is left untended, the longer a diaper goes unchanged, the greater the occurrence, and severity, of diaper rash. But Lara did not get diaper rashes there. I took this as evidence of good care. Really, it just meant she was cute, the star student in a very unlucky class.

Perhaps there was other evidence I should have looked for.

Intimidation was a standard and successful process used against parents and against the direct care staff. It even worked on me, a trained attorney, a courtroom litigator. And did I mention I was from Brooklyn? A naturally aggressive and fearless person, trained in street toughness, trained again for courtroom battle, that was me.

But they managed to scare the hell out of me. Regularly.

Intimidation was integrated into every aspect of the institution. Lara resided in Building 14, a one-story structure a few hundred feet wide. You would enter the building from a door in the center and pass to a narrow waiting room. From there, two halls, one to the left and one to the right, led to the two wards. Parents were "asked" to wait in the waiting room for the delivery of their child by one of the attendants, though this "request" had the tone of "would the prisoners please empty their pockets."

Although there were no longer regimented visiting hours, an ancient sign declared:

VISITING HOURS
Sundays and Wednesdays
1 to 4 P.M.
Other days by appointment

If no one was required to comply with the terms of the sign, its sole purpose must have been to reinforce the palpable atmosphere of intimidation. It worked.

Soon after we could visit Lara, I went to see her at Building 14. Initially, I obeyed the request that I wait for her in the waiting room. But I was anxious to see her. The clock ticked and I tapped my fingers on my chair and checked my watch, paced back and forth in the waiting room and wondered if they had forgotten me. Finally, I strode down the corridor and past the nurses' office towards Lara's ward. Suddenly, a loud, powerful voice surrounded me.

"Where do you think you're going!"

It was not a question. It was a demand, made by a rather large blonde nurse. She appeared to me to be a red-dogging linebacker. I stopped cold as I felt a chill ripple up my back and through my guts. I did not argue. I did not respond. I sure did not object. I made my best high school gym "about face," and marched back to my chair in the waiting room. I felt embarrassed and humiliated.

A nurse intimidated me. Willowbrook intimidated me. Murray the street tough. Murray the litigator. If they could intimidate me, they could intimidate any parent.

And what could they do to a child?

That would have been a good time to grab my daughter and run. But not yet. Things had to get much worse.

4

BSRC

One evening in September of 1969, Vicki and I were in bed. She had a smile on her face and so did I. It was hard not to smile. We had just learned that we were going to be parents again. The new baby was expected in late April 1970 and Lara had been in Willowbrook for less than two months. I was preparing questions for a deposition in a commercial litigation case I had the next day. I had promised myself that I would never do legal work in bed, but it was either read in bed or read in the kitchen, alone. The fresh heartbreak around Lara somehow signaled to me that I was not going to be the kind of husband and father who spends his life saying, "Not now, I'm working."

We had learned, with both joy and apprehension, that Vicki became pregnant the weekend we went away, the weekend we left Lara at Willowbrook. The news filled us with a sense of "starting over" and of joy and guilt. Would I love the new baby as much as I loved Lara? Would I forget about Lara when the new baby arrived? What kind of father was I, really?

Vicki was reading a brochure. "This is good," she said.

"What is it?"

"The parent organization. The Benevolent Society for Retarded Children."

"Nothing doing," I said.

She folded the brochure and laid it on her growing belly. "Why not?"

"I hate the word 'benevolent'. 'Benevolent' sounds like you're trying to fake someone out or kiss someone's ass. Those places are not for me."

The word "benevolent" was just an excuse and she knew it. I did not want to join the parents' group or any other group. I did not want to give away my independence, or feel like I lost my voice, like it got drowned in the crowd. I liked dinners for two. She liked big parties, the more the merrier. And why were the other parents my responsibility? Or their kids? Let them take care of their kids. I would take care of mine. That is what I cared about.

I focused on my child, my family. I had to make money and lots of it. I had a good practice but I had to make it grow. And every year had to be better than the year before. No slacking off. Worse, I had 31 years on Lara. I would have to set things up so she would be okay long after I was gone, even after Vicki was gone. There had to be medical care, a trust and a legal guardian who would be careful with that trust. So much to plan! I would never forget my promise.

But late at night, after the office was closed, my books and papers put away and the dishes were done, after the planning and the worrying that served to keep my brain occupied, when I got too tired to think, that is when I got angry.

Night after night, the same gut wrenching questions aimed at the stars: Why Lara instead of me? Why punish her and not me? Why punish my innocent child? And finally, what did I do to deserve this? I could not think of what I could have done that would justify such punishment, but still the feeling persisted, that she was punished for my horrible, unknown crimes.

I was an aggressive person who would take necessary action to correct a wrong. It was not that I had no fear. The big blonde nurse proved that. But I had been trained. Do what you have to do, even in the face of fear. *Especially* in the face of fear. I believe that all people are fearful in their daily lives and that such fear affects their behavior. Often the parents of mentally retarded children at Willowbrook, and other institutions, were extremely fearful, accentuated by the fact that their retarded children were living in miserable state institutions. They were afraid to anger their children's caretakers. They were afraid to make matters worse.

I could see this. I had the training in critical thinking to analyze facts and circumstances in order to determine what was actually real and realistic. I was logical and, although I was not fearless, I could behave as if I felt no fear.

Despite my misgivings, Vicki still insisted that I had something to offer the group.

When we first met with the parent organization— Benevolent Society for Good Will to Children (BSRC), "the Benevolents"—I noticed that most of parents were much older than I was. I was in my early 30s and most of them were in the 50s, 60s and 70s. I remembered that retarded children essentially remain children throughout their lives. So a couple in their 70s have the same child, emotionally, that they had 50 years ago. The parents were very happy to see us arrive. I did not know or recognize any of them from the institution.

"Welcome!" said Shirley Epstein, a board member.

"Come on in! Make yourselves at home."

"Have a seat!"

"There's bagels and coffee!"

"We need some new blood."

They did. They seemed to be in need and to be lost. They were unclear on how to run a meeting, let alone on how to plan action.

The meeting room was a big square, perhaps 40 feet by 40 feet. A long, narrow table sat at the front of the room, with four chairs behind it and ten rows of chairs facing it. That was the extent of the order in the meeting.

"Someone yelled at me."

"My kid has diaper rash."

"My son's eye and ear were injured but no one knows how it happened. And the direct care staff doesn't care."

"The nurse told me that my daughter fell and her head needed three stitches. Her eye was black and blue. And Bessie can't walk. They move her in a wheelchair or a cripple cart. Last winter she got second degree burns on her arm and leg because of those damn uncovered radiators."

They wanted to tell me of the conditions their children faced. They drew me right in.

What can I say? I felt needed. What I saw in Lara's Building 14 seemed to be an oasis.

They were not lawyers, or advocates, or particularly analytical. They were frustrated and angry, but that did not get them anywhere. Mostly, they were afraid. They were afraid of the administration. They were afraid to complain to anyone in authority. And they were specifically afraid for the well being of their own children.

Another warning I missed: parents giving less thought to a child's progress than to the possibility of harm that might come to that child at the hands of caretakers.

As the meeting broke up, we were approached by Tony Pinto. Tony was a Captain in the New York City Fire Department. He was considerably older than me. His white hair did little to hide the fact that he was built like a bull. I learned that as a Captain he was the first firefighter into every burning building. He introduced himself and then nodded at the chair and co-chair. "They use their positions to suck up to the school director. Fools!"

I quickly assessed the chair and co-chair. I was reminded of the Jews used by the Nazis to shepherd other Jews into the concentration camps. They thought they would be saved, and they were, for a time. They were the last ones to be gassed.

At my first chance after that meeting, I did some research. The director of the Willowbrook State School, I learned, was Dr. Jack Hammond, a psychiatrist. He was tall and chubby with pale skin and a narrow, pointed face. I learned that virtually all of the directors of the New York State institutions for the mentally retarded were psychiatrists. At first glance this seems to make perfect sense. It only seems odd when you learn that *psychiatrists were never utilized in such institutions for the mentally retarded.* Those living in the institutions for the mentally retarded were provided no psychiatric services. As a euphemism, they were named "State Schools" but no one was taught very much and no one ever graduated, except in a wooden box. Sure, you would expect therapists, teachers, doctors and nurses but why psychiatrists? The almost universal employment of psychiatrists in chief administrator positions struck me as very strange. I mentioned it to Vicki.

"Could it be a coincidence? An accident?"

"I don't believe in accidents. Looks more like a plan."

She raised an eyebrow and grinned. "A conspiracy?"

"Sure, I'm paranoid. Or I'm right. Either way, this is deliberate."

I listened to people whose judgment I trusted: a few other lawyers and judges, and my wife. But, mostly, I trusted my instincts, my gut, even my nose. And I smelled a rat.

Since no psychiatric services were provided to any Willowbrook resident, Dr. Hammond and his kind were hired for another reason. I kept thinking of the sign on the wall: **VISITING HOURS Sundays and Wednesdays, 1 to 4 P.M.** Bold and intimidating. And the waiting room where even the parents were confined, and not permitting us to visit Lara for the first 30 days. If Tony Pinto was right, the leaders of the parents' organization, the Benevolents, used their status to buddy up to Dr. Hammond, hoping to secure good treatment for their own children. They seemed motivated not just by selfishness but by fear. And given the fact that conditions were extensively miserable for both the residents and the direct care providers, keeping the parents quiet and the staff under control had to be a major concern. I came to the conclusion that psychiatrists were employed to best manipulate the parents and staff, to keep us all in line.

I could not have admitted this then, but during this period of time I was always afraid, fear was my shadow. This was not a boxing ring. If I came out swinging, the risk was not a broken nose for me but something horrible happening to Lara. I had to be a different kind of tough, a different kind of brave. I would think about this as I held Lara and sang to her and tried to make her feel secure. What did "brave" mean? I did not have to cower just because I was scared. I would never admit that I was afraid but I could hold my fear so close that no one could ever detect it.

The fight for dignity and truth fortifies your soul and prepares you for the next challenge.

It would come before I knew it.

5

ELIZABETH

When Vicki became pregnant for the second time, I insisted that her new doctor be an OB/GYN who was a highly experienced and skilled surgeon. Vicki said, "You have your demands, I have mine. No pain."

"Okay."

"I mean it. None. You want to see natural labor, go through it yourself."

The doctor went along with her plan: caesarian section *before* Vicki was set to go into labor.

"Fair enough," the doctor said.

"And one more thing," I said. "The baby goes straight into pediatric intensive care until we're sure there are no breathing problems, no blood problems, no problems period!"

"Agreed," he said.

It was good to have a competent physician who heard what you had to say.

In her hospital room, Vicki was supposed to change into a hospital gown. But it was not her style. So when they came for her, she was striding around the room in full make-up, fluttering her false eyelashes. Her huge, protuberant stomach pushed out the front of her hot pink negligee, and her hot pink feather boa flowed in her wake.

At the time, I thought she was being funny. I wondered later if she was making sure that her second time giving birth would be nothing—absolutely nothing—like her first. Of course, before she was prepped for the delivery, the make-up, false eyelashes, negligee and boa had to be retired until after the delivery. She was not happy. I laughed.

I had my own worries. Would the baby be all right? Would Vicki? With a normal baby, would I love Lara any less? I waited in the waiting room as best as I could.

"Mr. Schneps? It's a girl."

She was gorgeous with a beautiful face, rosy silky skin, peach fuzz orange hair and had no red spot on her forehead. She was awake making some sounds and her mouth was searching for food. She was perfect.

And I felt at that moment that my heart was big enough to have room for the new baby, and Lara, and whoever else might come along.

For her birth announcement we let everyone know that:

"We Are Proud to Welcome Lara's New Sister, Elizabeth Joy."

It was just a little while later, on a cool day in September 1970, that I met a man who would have a great influence over my life, though I would be hard pressed to explain the nature of that influence.

Elizabeth was five months old and Vicki and I were driving to Willowbrook to visit Lara. When we approached the guard booth at the entrance I saw that the mechanical arm on the security gate was closed in its "down" position. This is unusual, I thought. I had never before seen the barrier closed. The gate was always open and only occasionally was a guard present. There was a dark blue Buick pulled up to the barrier, doors open, and three men standing by the guard's booth. It appeared as if the car and its passengers were being prevented from entering. With Lara living at Willowbrook almost full time, I had developed a proprietary feeling towards it. I told Vicki, "I'm gonna find out what's going on." I pulled over and got out.

The first man stood a head taller than me, hefty, with a great mane of red hair and a full red beard. The little skin on his face that I could see also flushed red (though it may have normally looked that way), owing, I guessed, to the fact that he was roaring a stream of epithets in a thick Irish brogue at the guard. With him stood a thinner man in a suit, and a third man carrying a large black box that I took to be a transmitter, basing my hunch on the microphone attached by a long wire.

When the Irishman seemed to halt for breath, I cut in. "Can I help?"

The Irishman noticed me. "I hope t' hell ye can. Malachy's the name. McCourt, that is. I host a radio show for WMCA in New York City. This is Bob....." (I didn't get the name) "my producer, and this scrappin' young lad here is ....." (ditto) "my sound man. We're trying to record a show broadcasting me astute observations and critiques about this excellent crap hole and its conditions."

This was the early days of the parent outcry against the horrible conditions existing at Willowbrook. As the Benevolents had appointed me as the chairman of the newly designated Action Committee, I dove into the fray. I approached the guard.

"I'm Murray Schneps. My wife and I are going to visit our daughter in Building 14. What's going on?"

"You can go in," he said.

"Why can't these other men enter?" I asked.

"They are not permitted to enter the property. Visiting privileges are for family members only."

Malachy burst out. "My stepdaughter lives in this shit shack, ya fascist whelp!"

I raised a palm in Malachy's direction. He quieted.

I said, "These men are my guests and I am taking them with me to visit my daughter as well as other areas and buildings."

The guard pursed his lips, then picked up his phone. I took a few steps back to give him privacy.

He hung up, flipped a switch, and the barrier rose. Malachy's face lit with a smile and its color went from a pre-coronary red to an accommodating pink. He shook my hand heartily.

"Thank ye," he said. "In the car, lads."

"I hope I see you again," I said.

"Time will tell, friend. Time will tell."

As I got to know Malachy McCourt, I learned that he was a multifaceted man. A gifted raconteur, a restaurant owner, a radio host, a talented actor, playwright and author. But for me his most cherished role became one of friend and passionate collaborator on the side of truth and fairness. His red hair could match his coloring when his explosions of passionate rhetoric and poetry took hold. It was like being friends with a lyrical lion.

He used his radio show on WMCA in New York City as a platform for social discourse on injustices and abuse he felt or saw and we were lucky to have his early input into the conditions at Willowbrook.

6

GOUVERNEUR

It was a Sunday night in the spring of 1971. I was 33 and still had a full head of hair. I did not have gorgeous red hair like Lara and Elizabeth but I had hair.

Elizabeth was almost a year old. Vicki had gotten down to her pre-pregnancy weight. Lara was 3 years old and living in Willowbrook. Other than a few colds and three hospitalizations at New York University Hospital due to pneumonias, she appeared to be doing fine. Due to her breathing problems, I assumed and was led to believe that pneumonia was an anticipated complication. We had seen her that day in Building 14. Lara seemed well cared for.

I was reviewing some legal papers on the sofa and Vicki was playing with Elizabeth on the carpet when the kitchen phone rang. I said, "I got it."

"Hello?"

"Murray? It's Shirley Epstein, from the parent's organization."

She was one of the officers of the Benevolents, one of the ones who sucked up to Dr. Hammond. I usually listened to what she had to say as she always had a lot of information. She spoke with Dr. Hammond almost daily.

"Hello Shirley, what's going on?"

"Are you alone?" she asked.

I looked around. "Yeah, I'm... Shirley, what's up?"

"What do you know about Gouverneur Hospital?"

I knew a little about the place, owing mostly to the fact that it had been around since the turn of the century, and stood in Lower Manhattan, a stone's throw from my law office. The residents, like Lara, were profoundly retarded, multiply handicapped, mostly non-ambulatory, most could not speak and required constant supervision. I told her all this.

"What else do you know about them?"

"That they're poor and black or Puerto Rican. Anything else?"

"Did you know that they were transferred to Gouverneur to reduce overcrowding at Willowbrook?"

"No, I didn't."

"And I was told that they were sickly and expected to die so they were sent to Gouverneur from Willowbrook."

"So they sent them to die at Gouverneur?"

"Think about it."

"Are you kidding me?"

"No, I'm not. It's so they won't die at Willowbrook."

I screwed up my face in disbelief.

"Well, the plan got screwed up when the children didn't die. Best laid plans, right? Anyway," she went on, "maybe it was just an easy way to get rid of the blacks and

Puerto Ricans. I bet you never thought of Willowbrook as an exclusive school."

"Lucky us."

I looked into the living room. Vicki cuddled Elizabeth by the light of the TV. I could just enjoy the moment and pretend everything was okay. Lots of parents did.

I had almost laughed out loud when Shirley asked if I was alone. Was this how information was shared? Through secret phone calls and whispers? Details passed from one person to the next. We had tried to act as a group but our leadership slept with the enemy. And we could not act as individuals. It was too difficult, too much of an energy drain and too scary.

"They're closing it."

"What?"

"Gouverneur Hospital. Dr. Hammond told me. They're firing the whole staff."

"What happens to the residents?"

"That's what I'm saying," she shouted, *they're coming back to Willowbrook!*"

To a casual observer, it might seem that 200 more residents in a large institution of 5,700 mentally retarded individuals would be hardly noticed. But we knew better. Willowbrook was overcrowded and understaffed, the attendants overworked and heartsick. 200 more meant that corners would be cut. Feedings would be rushed. And Lara's feedings could not be rushed.

Children would die.

"Is this open for debate?" I asked.

"Dr. Hammond said no. That nothing could alter, amend or cancel the decision to close Gouverneur."

"That's what he said?"

"Those words exactly: alter, amend or cancel. The Gouverneur parents are already marching there, but I don't see how—"

"Will they be there tomorrow morning?"

"Yes. Why? It's over. There's nothing to do!"

I thought for a moment about my two daughters, and what kind of father I wanted to be.

I said, "I'll be there at eight a.m."

"But—"

I hung up and grinned at the phone.

Nothing can alter, amend, or cancel the decision to close Gouverneur!

Are they kidding me?

This was a challenge.

Do not challenge me, Dr. Hammond. You may be a psychiatrist. You may know how to bully people. But I know how to fight. It seems as if I had always been fighting. I could never accept unfairness and felt compelled to speak out.

First opened in 1885 in an abandoned police station, Gouverneur Hospital's original purpose was to address the overcrowded, unsanitary living conditions resulting from the population growth on the Lower East Side during the last decades of the 19th Century. Through the decades it served the needs of the various communities in the neighborhood. It was the first municipal hospital to establish a tuberculosis clinic.

So it was Gouverneur Hospital's most recent incarnation, as a facility for mentally retarded children, that was to be closed and its children returned to Willowbrook. When I arrived early Monday morning, the parents were marching outside the building and preventing entry.

The building was narrow, about six stories tall and the front actually touched the sidewalk. Rusty metal fire escapes hung off each story, ending at the second floor with a ladder to the ground. A tall black metal fence surrounded the building. Protesters marched outside and inside the fence. Some hoisted signs or fastened signs to the fence. The signs blared out, "WE WON'T GO," "WE WILL NOT LEAVE," "DR. MILLER HELP US HELP OUR CHILDREN," and "DO NOT MOVE OUR KIDS." There were quite a few young men, both outside and inside the fence, and in the building. When I arrived, I introduced myself around. "Does anyone know who's in charge?" A tall young man sporting army fatigues and shoulder-length hair pointed to a tiny, slim black woman, shaking a larger woman's hand. I waited my turn.

When she was free, she looked up to me with a smile.

"Excuse me," I said, though I had not interrupted. "Are you in charge?"

"I wouldn't go that far. I'm the president of the parent organization. I'm Willie Mae Goodman but you can call me 'Goody.'" She shook my hand. Her nickname made me think of Old Salem, witch hunts, and *The Crucible,* and I giggled and said, "I'm Murray Schneps. Please call me

Murray. My daughter's at Willowbrook. I heard about your situation and I thought I could help."

"What can you do?"

For a moment I went blank. Then, "I'm…I'm a lawyer. I hope to stop the transfer."

"Oh, thank you. We really need some help. They want to transfer our kids back to Willowbrook. We will not let our kids go back to Willowbrook. Please help us. Let me introduce you around."

Goody gave me a tour of the facility, walking along the fence. She introduced me to the young men, all dressed neatly but ready for action. They wore an assortment of clothing but I saw a lot of jeans, sweatshirts, sneakers, bandanas and hats. "This is Carlos, and Jimmy, and Santiago. This is Marcos. John. Boys, this is Murray."

They looked me over with my smooth-shaved over-30 face, in my standard office clothes of a navy blue suit, black shoes, white shirt, tie and overcoat. I was not really old enough to be their fathers but to them I was an old guy. I did not look particularly fierce or scary. Goody said, "these young men are all members of the Young Lords."

I knew of the Young Lords from news reports of their activities on behalf of the Spanish community in New York City.

One of the young men stepped forward, jaw first, and asked, "Who are you?"

Goody said, "he's a good man. He came here to help us. He volunteered."

"I'm a lawyer. My daughter lives in Willowbrook and I think that I can help."

"'Cause you're so nice?"

I took a breath. "No, I'm selfish. My daughter lives at Willowbrook and moving more children back to Willowbrook will harm my daughter. Two hundred more children to care for would be impossible."

"Impossible?"

"Fatal."

They looked me over a second time.

"Goody," one of the guys said, "This guy's all right."

They looked like street toughs but they were just young kids who were there to protect everyone, the mothers and fathers of the children, and to prevent the State from moving the children out of Gouverneur and into Willowbrook. But it did not take much to see an hour into the future. If they began moving the children, and the Young Lords got in the way, the police would be called. Under the circumstances, the New York Police Department was not well known for showing restraint.

I smiled all I could but the clock was ticking.

Goody introduced me to many of the families. "Murray, this is José, this is Ethel and her girl, Alma. Their son Ethan lives here in the hospital. Eric's brother lives here and this is my daughter Margaret. She also lives here. We will not let them move our kids and we will not agree to a transfer back to Willowbrook. We want to keep our staff intact. We love them and we need them." She knew the families. She knew each resident by their first name and the name of every staff person.

Goody and several other parents told me that, although Gouverneur was an old decrepit building, they had a great relationship with the staff, who provided excellent services and care to their children. At Gouverneur their children were safe, clean, happy and well. Absenteeism in Willowbrook was rampant but did not exist at Gouverneur.

"We know that if the kids go back to Willowbrook," she said, "they'll die."

We were interrupted by one of the members of the board of directors of the Benevolent Society for Retarded Children (BSRC). It had not occurred to me that the BSRC existed away from Willowbrook. His name was Irwin Bier. He was about 5'9", 165 pounds, had brown hair and a mustache, and was about 50 years old.

He said, "this closing isn't the only closing. The Department of Mental Hygiene is going to close the Sampson State School, upstate near Geneva."

I said, "I'm not even sure where that is."

"Exactly. The residents are older men and women. Their parents are gone. Most of them have no relatives or guardians. They haven't had visitors in years and that is why they were transferred to Sampson from other institutions. Those residents have no connection to the outside world. These are people who have been in the system since before there was a system. Can you imagine what places for the mentally retarded were like in 1910?"

Considering what I had seen this week, it was hard to imagine.

Irwin went on. "So the budgets of these two crappy hospitals—"

I cut him off. "Add up to exactly what the state wants to save this year."

"Equals the budgets of Gouverneur and Sampson, almost to the penny. And they figured there'd be no opposition from either place."

The State was right about Sampson but wrong about Gouverneur. The parents were not kidding around and neither was Goody. They were committed to stopping the movement of their kids to Willowbrook. To that end, they were devoted and fearless. And so were the Young Lords.

What they were not was bulletproof.

I got ahold of Goody, pulled the parents and the leaders of the Young Lords together, and had an impromptu meeting.

"I'll help," I said, and a half-dozen furrowed eyebrows told me not everyone could imagine how I might do that. "But on one condition. The Young Lords must agree to remain inside the building and not to stand outside, especially around the fence."

Some Young Lords leaned forward. "Why not?"

"Because you're young and Puerto Rican and the police consider you expendable. If the papers pick it up, they'll report 'gang members charged in scuffle with police.' Your bodies get carted off and, even worse, Gouverneur gets emptied out into Willowbrook, where those residents stand a far greater chance of dying of neglect. Get the point?"

They did.

I went on. "Only parents and relatives picket outside at the entrances. The police will not injure or physically touch any of them. Are we in agreement?" There were a few exchanged looks, but no objections. Just then, a few battered, old, large yellow school buses, with standard bus seats, pulled up in front of Gouverneur.

Most of the children were non-ambulatory and suffered extensive spasticity. There were not enough wheelchairs and there were no wheelchairs that had been adapted for any particular child. No head supports or limb adjustments existed to accommodate the children. Most often the children were moved by way of so-called "cripple carts." Cripple carts were wheeled platforms about five feet long by two to three feet wide, without seats or backs. The cripple carts were fabricated from old broken wheelchairs. They looked barbaric and more appropriate for moving corpses, not living children. Of course, it was cheaper to cannibalize a broken wheelchair to make a "cripple cart" and more efficient, since each cart could carry two or more kids. Appropriately adapted wheelchairs, to alleviate contractures and permit a child to sit upright, were not available at Gouverneur or Willowbrook.

The joke was on them. You could not possibly move these residents in regular school bus seats. To me, the presence of conventional buses showed how little the State knew or cared about the residents.

I asked Goody, several other parents and an employee, Terry, to accompany me to my office. I prepared an Order to Show Cause seeking to prevent the closing of Gouverneur

Hospital and the Sampson State School, to prevent the transfer of children or adults to any other facility, and to prevent the termination of any employees.

Normally, when you ask the court to prevent action by another party you must give that party notice that you are seeking to stop them. But if you can demonstrate good cause for the relief you seek, and also the probability of "irreparable harm" to your clients, you may seek such relief without prior notice to the other side. Based upon the parents' affidavits, the Court agreed that moving the children from Gouverneur and the adults from Sampson was such "irreparable harm" and we stopped the moves until the court could hear from both sides.

It was a temporary victory but seeing the useless old yellow school buses roll away from Gouverneur empty had us cheering.

I prepared for the hearing at my office, when I was supposed to be working on my real caseload, and at home, when I was supposed to be paying attention to Vicki and Elizabeth. Though only a year old, Elizabeth had flaming red hair, a bright, beautiful face and an outgoing personality. She would walk and dance and jump. How lucky we were! I sat at the kitchen table, notes and affidavits spread before me, preparing arguments, while Elizabeth made every effort to distract me.

Vicki said, "I've never seen you like this before," but it was not really a complaint. I was excited. It was my first litigation involving the mentally retarded.

At the oral argument of the Order to Show Cause, the courtroom was packed. I spotted Goody, many of the Gouverneur parents, and many others I could not identify. Irwin, who I met at Gouverneur, handed me an envelope.

"What's this?

It was addressed to me, care of the Benevolents, from an address in Geneva, New York.

"Open it."

Dear Mr. Schneps,

Please accept this to cover costs and disbursements you personally incurred. We wish it could be more.

So the residents of the Sampson State School were not entirely friendless. I am not inclined to blush, but when I saw that check, I felt as if I were in heaven. It was not huge, it would not even cover my costs. But it was a statement that people valued the work I was doing, work I believed in.

"Gonna bill them for more?" Irwin grinned.

"Murray!"

I turned. Sitting in front center of the audience was my dear cousin, Ruth Levine. I waved back, and dismissed Irwin's joke.

"Of course not," I said.

"Why not?"

I was still looking at Ruth. "She knows why."

Ruth's mother was my Aunt Miriam, my mother's oldest sister. Miriam Sheindel Kandel Fenichel Provorny. A lot of name but she was a lot of person. Miriam was my favorite aunt. When I was in college, I had called my aunt for a loan of two thousand dollars. In the mid-1950s that was a lot of money. To me, it was very serious money.

She said, "Meet me tomorrow morning at my bank at ten."

"Don't you want to know why I want to borrow so much money?"

"If you asked for that much money," she said, "you must need it."

When I graduated from law school, she gave me a note that said, simply, "Dear Murray, I am proud of you. Miriam." She never asked for the money, or for an IOU. She trusted me.

Of course, I repaid the loan. But there was more to the story than money. Miriam's actions influenced me.

No Irwin, I would not ask for any other money for the work I provided in that case.

I always felt comfortable engaging in legal argument. So, although I felt nervous, I knew that I was well prepared, fully committed, and was on the side of G-d and the angels, with my family sitting front and center. The oral argument went extremely well. I informed the Court, "two hundred severely and profoundly retarded multiply handicapped children will be sent to their deaths if transferred from the Gouverneur Hospital in lower Manhattan to Willowbrook State School in Staten Island. Such transfer will be the equivalent of transferring the Jews from their homes in Poland to the gas chambers of Auschwitz."

I think I got the Court's attention.

This was a "fact case." The first effort was to secure an injunction, which meant stopping the transfer of the

Gouverneur children to Willowbrook and retaining their staff, victory was for later. I presented a factual yet emotional case. The emptying of the residents of Gouverneur Hospital into the already overcrowded and understaffed Willowbrook State School presented a clear and immediate danger to the residents of both institutions. The fact that the residents in Gouverneur were children was helpful.

Actually, in those days, most people referred to the mentally retarded as children, to wit: the Benevolent Society for Retarded Children, the New York State Association for Retarded Children and the Working Organization for Retarded Children. I think referring to the mentally retarded as "children" made people feel better. Sometimes reality can be too painful to accept. Later, most agencies substituted the term "Citizens" for "Children," to retain their acronyms, to wit: BSRC, NYSARC and WORC.

My argument was energetic, emotional, smooth, and contained many inflammatory facts including the acceleration of serious injuries due to overcrowding and lack of adequate staff and the increased death rate especially among the profoundly retarded multiply handicapped children.

Here was the clincher: "I should point out that each institution was named, itemized, and included in the Budget Law and, accordingly, the Commissioner is not authorized to override a statute by eliminating a line item contained in the Budget Law." Each year a budget is enacted by the legislature. That budget is a statute. A statute or law must be complied with. The budget contains a listing of specific programs that will be paid for. Both

Gouverneur Hospital and the Sampson State School were specifically listed with the amount of money for appropriated to each, separately.

Game, set, and match.

The judge granted an injunction which barred the transfers of residents from either institution, the closing of either institution and the firing of any of the staff.

The room burst into cheers.

In the weeks to follow, the Department of Mental Hygiene, in layman's terms, "went nuts." The Commissioner, Dr. Alan Miller, and his Deputy, Dr. Frederic Grunberg, tried to cajole me into vacating the injunction with threats, both subtle and overt. They asked to meet with me at the Manhattan State School in lower Manhattan "to resolve the matter."

"Looks pretty resolved to me."

"We need to save money, Murray!" Dr. Miller pleaded.

I sighed. "I'll meet with you. That's all."

When I arrived at the conference room at the Manhattan State School, the two men were seated, but Dr. Miller rose, shook my hand, and said, "I have to leave but Dr. Grunberg will handle the matter."

I said, "You knew we were meeting today, right?"

Dr. Miller disappeared like he was dodging autograph seekers. I was none too happy. I did not like or trust Dr. Grunberg. Not that I liked or trusted Dr. Miller. But I knew Dr. Grunberg and disliked him for his blatant disregard for the residents and for his arrogant refusal to communicate with our side, whereas I was only beginning to dislike Dr. Miller.

As soon as we were alone, Dr. Grunberg said, "Murray, you must immediately vacate the injunction or my alternative plan will be far worse."

"Far worse?" I asked. "You're not bothered by cutting staff so much that children die at an alarming rate. What constitutes 'far worse'?"

He folded his arms.

"Dr. Grunberg," I asked, "why don't you just use our plan of cutting some of the top heavy administrators who provide no direct services to the residents? It's better than the Commissioner's plan." He simply smirked, stood and began to leave the room.

"Dr. Grunberg, sit down." He paused and then kept walking. I raised my voice and called at him, "Dr. Grunberg, leaving this room would not be wise."

I could make threats, too.

He stopped, spun around, returned to the table and sat down.

But he had run out of conversation. He had no authority and no real plans to negotiate.

Although the meeting ended without any resolution, we won the first round.

But on July 1, 1971, the Appellate Division, First Department, unanimously reversed the order and dismissed the case holding that the Commissioner had the power and authority to terminate a program without legislative approval. In spite of this, Gouverneur Hospital was not closed and none of the staff was terminated. How? Goody persisted. She refused to permit the moving of her "kids." She organized her community and got the support of local State legislators. Lucky kids.

I was glad to help. I was a good litigator but I was not Goody.

Just the same, the Sampson State School was promptly closed and its residents scattered to other institutions. I believe that most, if not all, of the Sampson employees were terminated. Of course, the Sampson residents did not have family or friends available or able to protect and represent them. And I did not have the resources to help them in upstate New York.

It was a sad commentary on the realities of this country, and a sad commentary on human nature and politics. When the economy soared, the State made at least some provision of necessary services for the neediest. But as soon as the economy declined, the cuts came from those with no power, as if the most needy were the least important. Suddenly, the neediest could be ignored, if only they could be moved out of sight.

The residents at Gouverneur, at Sampson and at Willowbrook were genuinely helpless. It might have been expedience that motivated their enemies, or power. But from where I stood, it looked like some bullies picking on a bunch of helpless kids. Kids like mine.

Not long thereafter, both Dr. Miller and Dr. Grunberg left the Department of Mental Hygiene. Obviously, Dr. Miller and Dr. Grunberg decided that they no longer wanted to deal with me and the other parents. Who needed the aggravation? Who needed to look like a villain? Too bad they did not leave us with the gift of admitting how truly terrible the conditions at the institutions were.

7

HOME AGAIN

The question came up over and over as I took on more cases involving the mentally retarded, some for full fee, some partial fee, some *pro bono*. Why? Why those cases? Why the late nights and the weekends? There were other cases, other worthy causes and certainly other cases that would bring in more money for my family.

The answer was, I could see my limits. I could not make Lara better. I could not make her talk or grow or see. But I could argue. I could use my brain, open my Brooklyn mouth and fight like a tiger. And most often I would win. If that made the world a slightly better place for Lara and people like her, well, that made me feel like a good dad.

In late 1969, America faced a severe economic downturn that affected the New York State budget in general and, specifically, the budget of the New York State Department of Mental Hygiene, which oversaw and operated Willowbrook and all other New York State institutions for the mentally retarded and the mentally ill. Belts had to be tightened, and whose belt was easiest to squeeze? Who was less likely to complain?

The State made some harsh decisions.

In 1969, Lara was 18 months old. She remained without speech while other babies her age were making sounds, non-ambulatory when babies her age were walking, and unable to sit without assistance or support her head. Worse, she had poor sucking and swallowing reflexes, which meant she had more trouble drinking from a bottle than a healthy newborn would. And she was not the only one at Willowbrook with such difficulties. Many residents suffered conditions that affected their ability to eat food effectively. Feeding them required time and patience. The process could take up to an hour to complete. Many residents were inadequately fed and, worse, others were force-fed by stuffing food into their mouths as quickly as possible. This caused aspiration of food into the lungs, resulting in pneumonia, choking and, at times, death.

But time, like everything, was regimented and limited in the wards and feeding was to take place in a period of one hour. Some of the less handicapped children could feed themselves but that still left two to four attendants a total of 60 minutes to feed 50 mouths, many of which required up to 60 minutes of attention each. The math did not work.

That was before the budget cuts.

Rather than firing direct care staff, the State simply ordered a job freeze which resulted in no new hiring. Except for the most committed, toughest and staunchest employees, the direct care staff was constantly changing. It was a heart-wrenching job. One day, I noticed a female attendant, a slim blond woman in her thirties. Her nametag identified her as Charlotte. She sat in a large plastic chair, cradling a boy, maybe four years old, but in diapers. I could tell by his struggle with the bottle that he had a sucking and swallowing problem similar to Lara's. And I noticed the attendant's loving gaze toward him.

"You love him," I said.

She looked up at me, tears in her eyes. "That's what kills me."

The attendants came to the job with little or no training, and got little or no support as time went on. They asked the administration for help.

"We need more staff," they said.

The answer came back, "sorry."

"We need training in all kinds of therapy."

"Sorry."

Even the most dedicated and empathic of the staff became disheartened when they had to care for more and more of the multi-handicapped residents with less and less help. If anything, the ones with the biggest hearts burned out the fastest. They could not stand the daily heartbreak. Half the time they quit the same way, they phoned in on a Monday morning, or whenever their workweek began, sobbing and saying, "I can't. I just can't."

Who could blame them?

With the anticipated quitting and no new hires, the staff roster plummeted. Worse, that wards were so understaffed, it increased the pressure on remaining staff and, predictably, encouraged more of them to quit. As the economy slumped and staff continued to quit, without replacements, it soon reached the point where there were not nearly enough staff to properly assist the residents who could not feed themselves. Staff coverage grew thin, threatening the lives of those most fragile. Even Dr. Hammond stated publicly that he was no longer able to assure that the most fragile residents would survive.

The most fragile residents like Lara.

Lara was wholly dependent in all areas. In May of 1970, at two years of age, she was as helpless as a newborn. Throughout 1970 and 1971, and into 1972, conditions at Willowbrook continued to deteriorate. Lara still never had a diaper rash but the staff struggled harder and harder to maintain good services and their sanity. Their jobs were not for sissies.

On February 18, 1972, we brought Lara home for the weekend. We enjoyed a nice weekend with both our girls and were hoping we could add to our family soon. We were feeling optimistic that Sunday afternoon as we drove back to Staten Island to the imposing grounds of Willowbrook to return her to the ward. I slowed the car as we entered the Willowbrook grounds and I caught the image of a beam of afternoon sun hitting Lara's red hair as she dozed, cuddled in Vicki's arms. Along with failing to grow mentally, she had failed to grow physically. At three and a half years old, she remained quite small, the size of a small one-year-old. I wondered if I could just pretend she was a baby forever.

When we arrived at Building 14 we found that there was only one staff member to feed, diaper, and otherwise care for the 100 babies in her care. Half of them were howling and, if smell was any indicator, a third of them needed changing. I realized the one staff member was

Charlotte, the blond woman who I had seen feeding the four-year-old boy in diapers. The woman with the big heart. She stood between two wards—50 beds each—crying.

"Don't leave her here. Please!"

"Charlotte," I said, "where is everyone?"

"This is it," she cried. "It's just me!" We could barely hear her over the crying babies as she sobbed, "what's gonna happen?"

Vicki took her aside. "Shh, what's most urgent, food or diapers?"

Charlotte thought for a moment. "Right now? Diapers."

"Who needs it most?" Charlotte pointed.

"Then lets change those children first."

I said, "What about the next ward over?"

Charlotte whimpered. "One attendant, just like me, covering two wards!"

I went over to verify. Same scene. A hundred crying babies, and one panicked adult. I said, "Hold tight," and ran back to Ward B.

Vicki was giving a bottle to a child as Charlotte changed diapers. I said, "Who's the administrator on duty right now?"

Charlotte said, "Mr. Meizler. Extension 4857. But he's very difficult."

"Uh-huh." I grabbed the wall phone and dialed.

He answered on the fifth ring. "Alan Meizler."

"This is Murray Schneps. My daughter is a resident in Ward B in Building 14. You might not know but you have four wards here with 50 babies each, all under the care of two attendants. Get it?"

"What…"

"Each attendant is covering two wards with 100 babies each. What the hell is going on here? Are you trying to kill these children?"

"Well—"

"Stop talking. Get enough staff over here to cover these wards, now. And get over here and see what's going on. A lawsuit may be filed any minute. Oh, Mr. Meizler?"

"Yes?"

"I'm a lawyer."

I hung up and turned to Vicki. "As soon as the additional staff and Mr. Meizner get here, let's get Lara the hell out of here."

"Sure," she said, "as soon as things are under control."

Vicki was right. Just because we would never permit Lara to live under these conditions, there was no reason to abandon the children who could not leave. How lucky we really were. We had options. I was seconds away from taking my baby home and forgetting that horrible place, wiping it from my memory like a bad dream, and saying "tough luck!" to all the poor bastards who got stuck there. But we needed to go a step farther.

Finally, when Mr. Meizner and relief arrived and got things organized, we scooped up our baby and took her home. Away from Willowbrook for good.

So sorry baby girl. So sorry I left you there.

We had solved our own problem, at least for the moment. And that is what mattered, was it not?

8

THE STRIKE

But back at Willowbrook, troubles continued to grow for the direct care staff. The budget cuts continued and wards continued to be overcrowded and understaffed, so the remaining staff was ever more overworked. And underpaid. This group included attendants and nurses. Finally, their union decided to strike.

Direct care workers—nurses, attendants and therapists—"walked out" of Willowbrook on March 31, 1972, the Friday before Easter Sunday, and began marching around the main building, to the chagrin of the administration. Administrators covered the wards but there were not enough of them, and they lacked the skills and the inclination to care for, clean and feed the residents. The State did not bring in nonunion workers to fill in for the lost direct care workers. I can only guess that they saw the strike as an opportunity to save money: as long as the staff was striking, the strikers were not paid.

The employees and their union sought to restore the budget cuts and adequate numbers of staff to cover the overcrowded wards. Essentially, this was a cry for help and an effort to bring attention to the deteriorating conditions caused by the budget cuts. Fortunately, approximately one-half of the direct care workers came to work and hundreds of volunteers spontaneously appeared. A few of the Benevolents and some unaffiliated parents came to their children's respective buildings to check how their children were doing. I drove to Willowbrook and visited the residential buildings and wards to make sure there was coverage for all of the residents. I was appalled, but not surprised, to see Shirley Epstein and some of the parent leaders from the Benevolent Society sitting with Dr. Hammond in his office and commiserating with him. Poor, poor Dr. Hammond.

"This isn't local," Shirley told me. "All the state schools for the mentally retarded had walk outs."

TV cameras rolled. All the TV news programs reported the strike at Willowbrook. Little, if any, attention was being focused on any other institution. Why did we get the press?

Flash back a few months.

The Young Lords was a Puerto Rican nationalist group, also known as the Young Lords Party and the Young Lords Organization, founded in Chicago, Illinois. On January 8, 1970, 106 followers and supporters of the Young Lords took over the First Spanish Methodist Church in East Harlem, New York, and were arrested. Michael Wilkins, M.D., one of the supporters, was arrested with them.

A young lawyer, a recent graduate of my alma mater, Brooklyn Law School, represented the 106 occupiers/ demonstrators, including Dr. Wilkins.

He was young, brash, and much too hip for an industry that still featured the likes of Walter Cronkite. But Al Primo at ABC-TV heard Gerald speaking for the Young Lords, thought ABC could use a Puerto Rican TV journalist, offered him more than he was making as a lawyer, ($300 a week to start, instead of $200) and suggested a modification to his name. Gerald became Geraldo, the name already employed by his Puerto Rican father but not by his Jewish mother, and a legend was born.

Enter Geraldo Rivera.

It was during the Young Lords story that the arrested doctor, Michael Wilkins, and the half-Jewish half-Puerto Rican lawyer turned Puerto Rican TV journalist, Geraldo Rivera, became friends. In August 1970, Mike started working at Willowbrook as a physician. His work provided him with a rude education. In November and December 1971, he and a social worker, Elizabeth Lee, began to meet with some parents to assist them in actively advocating for their children. They were fired in January 1972. Upon being fired, Mike called Geraldo, already an ABC TV newsman, to invite and urge him to see Willowbrook in all its horrific glory. On a frigid winter morning, Mike secretly guided Geraldo and his film crew on a tour of Willowbrook to witness and document the degradation visited upon all who resided and worked in Building 6.

Geraldo's stories were broadcast throughout the area surrounding New York City and beyond. Not just once but continually and daily. No one who watched the news in the winter of 1971/1972 could ignore the conditions at Willowbrook.

Geraldo Rivera's first report from Willowbrook on January 10, 1972, included these words:

"There was one attendant for perhaps 50 severely and profoundly retarded children. Lying on the floor, naked and smeared with their own feces, they were making a pitiful sound, a kind of mournful wail that it is impossible for me to forget. This is what it looked like, this is what it sounded like but how can I tell you about the way it smelled? It smelled of filth, it smelled of disease, and it smelled of death."

Geraldo told Dr. Wilkins that the building he visited was the most horrible thing he had ever seen in his life and asked whether that was typical of ward life at Willowbrook. Dr Wilkins responded:

"Yes, there are 5300 patients at Willowbrook, which is the largest institution for the mentally retarded in the world. The ones that we saw were the most severely and profoundly retarded. There are thousands of them like that, not going to school, sitting on the ward all day, not being talked to by anyone, only one or two or three people to take care of 70 people on the ward."

We watched the report and the accompanying film footage in horror. It was painful to hear Geraldo's unadorned truth. Until then I had focused on Lara's Building 14 – I had a bad case of tunnel vision regarding her condition. Since she was clean, without injuries, without diaper rashes, it was basically tolerable. I had not considered the conditions in the other residential buildings in Willowbrook, or for that matter, even in Lara's own ward. Lara's ward had been crowded, sure, with 50 white metal cribs lined up within a couple of feet of each other. The room was gray and dull and drab but Lara was blind. There was the hard gray terrazzo floor and the pervasive mustiness with a slight stink of urine and feces. After visits, the smell attached to your clothing. But with 50 kids in diapers, it was to be expected. Wasn't it?

Somehow, the fact that we had made a decision to place Lara in Willowbrook affected my judgment and all other decisions. It was as if that decision had to protect itself. There was no better option. Therefore, Willowbrook was the only acceptable option. That is why we put her there. Therefore, she must belong there.

We needed her to be safe. Therefore, she was safe. We had brought her to Willowbrook to be safe. Therefore, the matter was settled. Until now.

No one who ever visited any of the buildings at Willowbrook with eyes, ears, and a nose could dispute Geraldo's evaluation. I started finding excuses to visit other wards in the hospital, the wards for young children, older children, young adults, and older adults.

Security was not a problem.

Those other buildings made the baby buildings look like heaven. How truly sad that statement is because, in reality, the baby buildings were closer to hell than to heaven.

The other buildings held wards of anywhere from 40 to more than 70 residents each. Male and female residents in various states of undress, many completely undressed, wandered about unsupervised. Some sat in the few plastic chairs present, others lay on the hard terrazzo floors, which were filthy with urine and feces. The toilets were an abomination of filth, installed in a row without walls or other separations between them. And the toilets and the wards smelled of ungodly foulness. Before these visits, I had never experienced such a stink. In addition to the darkness, there was the dankness, the stench, the lack of clothing or furniture or structure of any kind, and moans and screams penetrated and pierced all the wards. The residents were simply our fellow human beings who were forced to live in an inhuman environment.

I learned later that Robert Kennedy had visited the hospital seven years earlier, in 1965. He framed the hospital in terms of the title of a psychiatric hospital in a 1948 Olivia de Havilland movie. He called Willowbrook a "Snake Pit."

I saw that film. Olivia de Havilland had it easy.

Geraldo showed the real story.

So when the strike came, covered as it was by Geraldo in his poetic prose, cars rolled into the parking lot from all over the state and the country. Hundreds of volunteers arrived to assist taking care of the unattended residents. Where each ward had two or three direct care employees prior to the strike, now each ward had ten or more volunteers. Several of the parents and I led the charge, organizing schedules, making charts, going from building to building and ward to ward to make sure all the residents were tended to. It did not take much to see that the wards were running more smoothly now than they had before. Obviously, they had more hands on deck. Somehow the fact that a ward was being run by parents made it work differently. It was as if the system suddenly had a heart.

But it was a statewide strike and only Willowbrook got the press. Other institutions got only a smattering of volunteers, while we got hundreds and hundreds of volunteers on a seemingly endless stream.

It pays to advertise.

We were of mixed emotions, the other parents and Vicki and I. We wanted the strike to be successful. We wanted better working conditions for the direct care workers. We wanted them well paid, well supplied, well trained, properly staffed (that is, not overworked), and appreciated but we could not leave the children alone.

"We're strikebreakers," I said, feeding a small boy his bottle while my own daughter was safe at home. Lara's health had been stable since she was home and we were feeling hopeful.

Vicki called us "goodhearted strikebreakers."

Behind the reinforced glass of the administrative offices, I could still see some of the parents, even some of the Benevolents, sitting with Dr. Hammond. I could not hear the words but I could see the postures. Hammond slouched slightly and deliberately. He seemed distressed. Four parents sat around him, leaning close. Their expressions indicated that their greatest concern was the well being of the poor man at the center. Shirley actually patted his hand. I realized I was standing in full view of the office, staring, my mouth agape. But just before I made my escape, Dr. Hammond looked up and the others followed his gaze. Shirley jumped out of her chair. Shirley was a long-standing member of the board of directors of the BSRC. She was a "big macher," a big shot in Yiddish. She chased me out into the hall. I kept walking.

"Murray!" she called.

"I'm busy, Shirley."

"*Murray.*" She switched to a softer tone, one that was supposed to comfort me. It did not. I stopped and spun around in the narrow hall. She must have thought I was smiling. In reality, I was baring my teeth.

"*Shirley.*"

"Can we talk?"

A few words crossed my mind, most of them profane, the rest violent. I said, "Talk."

"We think it's wonderful what you're doing."

I cleared my throat. "By 'we' you mean your very peculiar alliance with management?"

"We don't see it that way."

"If I had Dr. Hammond's rear end covering my eyes, I would have trouble seeing much of anything, too."

"What do you think is gonna happen, Murray? When the strike's over? The children are used to all this attention and things go back to normal?"

I almost choked. I was too angry for a clever retort. Shirley was in Dr. Hammond's pocket. She was spouting

Hammond's arguments, Hammond's psychiatrist arguments. Hammond did not need anyone patting his hand.

"Shirley" I said. "There are hundreds of wards in this institution with a total of more than 5,700 residents. I have today and tomorrow to make sure everyone gets fed and changed because Monday I have to go to work. What are you doing, Shirley? When you are not kissing Hammond's ass, that is?"

"Me? I'm a bookkeeper. Why?"

"Not a psychiatrist?"

"No."

"Because you're so much like Dr. Hammond!"

The strike ended on Monday, April 3, 1972, the day after Easter Sunday. The residents and the staff enjoyed two great days with plenty of support, loving attention and care. Some residents even laughed out loud, a sound I had not heard there before. At the end of the strike things went back to the deprivation that was Willowbrook. Nothing changed. No improvements were secured. The budget remained unchanged and the residents continued to suffer.

The State of New York established residential institutions for the mentally retarded on State land, funded and operated the institutions with State employees, and exclusively provided what passed for day programs and services to the severely and profoundly mentally retarded residents of the institutions. The State was able to fill its institutions because it deliberately saw to it that few, if any, programs or services for such people were available outside of its institutions. If they wanted services, they had to be admitted as a resident. Most of the tax dollars were committed to maintaining the buildings that comprised the large institutions.

Only a tiny amount was set aside for the creation of group homes (some agencies referred to them as "hostels,") or day programs to provide for those living with their families. The severely and profoundly retarded were targeted and funneled into the large institutions. If a parent wanted services for his or her profoundly or severely retarded child, especially if the child was multiply handicapped (for example, retarded and blind, like Lara), there was no local option. No services in the community were available for such children. The institution was the exclusive provider of such services. The public schools afforded no services to such children in spite of the fact that all children were entitled to a free public education.

Parents of retarded children, especially of severely and profoundly retarded children, found themselves in a dilemma. No matter how reluctant they were to admit their child to an institution, there was no alternative. Worse, if you were worried about your child's care *after* your lifetime, the only answer was placement in a State institution. Logic, fairness, and morality would necessarily lead to a conclusion that the State would fulfill the obligations it had contracted for with these parents and their children, and assure adequate funding and services to maintain and protect those children throughout their lives.

But when it came down to the day-to-day care of thousands of disabled children and adults at multiple institutions across the State, the State of New York opted not to fulfill its obligations and morality went down the toilet. Once the budget was cut, an inevitable deterioration of all services immediately followed. The loss of direct care staff through attrition eroded all programs and services, including the proper feeding of those unable to feed themselves.

Of course, the parents were angry, disappointed, and fearful. New York State had double-crossed them. I hated the fact that the State had power over me but I was caught in its web. While I did the best that I could to fight back, I was always fearful and concerned about Lara's welfare. Case in point: I accused Dr. Hammond of refusing to fight for the rights of his charges. "You're the boss," I said, "but you're afraid to speak out." It was a calculated risk. At his core, Dr. Hammond wanted better treatment for his residents. But he wanted to keep his job. I thought I could goad him into taking action.

Not long after Geraldo's first visit to Willowbrook but before the strike, I learned that someone had moved Lara's crib from the entry area to the distant bowels of the ward. A child in a crib near the entry to the ward is easily seen and regularly observed. It was a privileged spot. Elsewhere a child could easily be over looked. I guessed Hammond had given the order in retaliation for my jabs at him. I considered the options: back down, beg him to reconsider or call Geraldo Rivera.

Geraldo showed up with his cameras.

When Hammond arrived, I confronted him. "Dr. Hammond, for the viewers of ABC-TV, would you justify the moving of my daughter, Lara Schneps?"

"Face the cameras, not me," he shouted. "That's what you want."

"You're full of shit!" I told him, diplomatically, as the cameras rolled. "I want to talk to you! In order to get at me, you are threatening my child. You are responsible for my child's welfare and I will make you accountable. I hold you personally responsible for her wellbeing and safety."

Lara's crib was promptly returned to its original location. The direct care staff continued to fawn over her, talk to her and cuddle her at every opportunity.

We were lucky, others were not.

As with most strikes, this one was settled and the staff, the ones who did not quit, went back to work. The direct care attendants had little power and not much changed.

Of course, I contemplated that I had cursed the leaders of the Benevolents for sucking up to Dr. Hammond for the benefit of their own children and then I promptly called Geraldo Rivera to help me maintain a privileged spot for my daughter on the ward. Although I was being a hypocrite my fear won out, so I had no regrets.

As the budget crisis persisted, the conditions at Willowbrook became intolerable. Geraldo Rivera was very articulate on the subject:

"Perhaps the Governor can defend and explain away the budget cuts of the Department of Mental Hygiene and perhaps Dr. Miller can explain and defend the filthy dehumanizing conditions we found in this place and other buildings but they won't do it on this program. What we found and documented here is a disgrace to all of us. This place isn't a school. It's a dark corner where we throw children who aren't pretty to look at. It's the big town's leper colony."

Sadly, protests by the parents, even when buoyed by the support of the media, were insufficient to turn the tide and protect the more than 5,700 mentally retarded individuals who remained at Willowbrook. A new chapter to force change was necessary.

9

NOT THE ONLY ONE

Back in 1971, when Dr. Michael Wilkins and Elizabeth Lee were fired for supporting and encouraging a group of activist parents, State budgets had been cut below austerity level. Willowbrook could barely function, not that it had functioned that well before. And firing employees who wanted the residents of Willowbrook to receive adequate care defied logic.

In response to the firings, Tony Pinto and I met and decided to prepare a list of demands:

1. The immediate reinstatement of Dr. Michael Wilkins and Mrs. Elizabeth Lee as employees at Willowbrook State School;

2. Providing written charges against them, if any exist;

3. If no written charges, permanent rehiring of them;

4. If written charges, an open hearing before independent panel (e.g. American Arbitration Association rules) with parent participation;

5. No further suspensions or firings in Social Services and Physicians without written charges to each employee and BSRC and available to all parents with an opportunity for open hearings by an independent panel including parents;

6. Acknowledgments to the principal of parent's meaningful active participation (BSRC) in administration and delivery of care, etc., with full access to all reports;

7. Immediate revocation of directions to any and all personnel restraining their contacts, of all kinds, with parents, individually and as groups with no impediments;

8. The issuance of a Policy Statement supporting full contact between parents and staff and administration and the parents and staff and parents and residents with no impediments;

9. A demand to lift the employee freeze and replace all lost staff to the December 1970 levels;

10. The State to issue a declaration of a disaster area at Willowbrook and request Federal and State emergency funds and assistance.

We mailed the demands to the Governor, and to the Commissioner of the Department of Mental Hygiene, with copies to Jerry Weingold and Robert Hodgson, respectively, as Executive Director and President of the

New York State Association for Retarded Children (NYSARC). Mr. Hodgson's reply on behalf of NYSARC, refused help, belittled our tactics and compared us to the Viet Cong, thus marking the first and last time a Pinto and a Schneps were compared to the Viet Cong.

Sadly, Tony Pinto returned the letter to Mr. Hodgson at Jerry Weingold's request, without retaining a copy. It would have made a nice keepsake.

Tony's heart was in the right place. I knew that when we wrote the list of demands together. But what he wanted was a cleaner Willowbrook with more staff. This difference between us came to a head one day as we were walking near the Administration Building.

"You don't understand," I said. "These places just don't work. My Lara could have died here."

He glared at me hard and began to shake. I did not know if he was about to yell or to cry. "My daughter died here!"

"What?"

"She couldn't stay with us. She needed an institution. People like her can only live safely in institutions. And I worried about what would happen when I died and who would take care of my little girl. We had no choice."

I opened my mouth but had nothing to say. "I'm...I'm sorry."

"So stop acting so self-righteous. Some people just want their kid to be safe. You're not the only one."

"I'm sorry."

"You're not the only one," he almost whispered as he turned and walked away.

Tony was a committed man. I learned later that he would frequently roam the halls and buildings of Willowbrook, looking into the wards, as if waiting for a small ghost to appear. Poor Tony, I vowed that that would never be me.

I liked Tony and I respected him. But I knew that we were not walking the same road. Tony wanted a better Willowbrook. I wanted to eliminate all Willowbrooks. I knew that small community homes were the only path.

In the final analysis, the NYSARC, Jerry Weingold, Helen Kaplan, and Robert Hodgson were more politicians than advocates. They worked, operated, constructed, and built upon compromise. Politicians are required to compromise but they have no place in the battle for civil rights. They have to please and satisfy too many bosses, too many managers, and too many loyalties. I recognize their need but I could not perform that job. I would not step into their theater and they should not step into mine. For me, it was all simple, uncomplicated, and singular: what was in the best interests of my child?

10

THE CLASS ACTION

Lara had not been home more than a few days. Her presence changed us. She required constant attention. But her spasticity seemed to relax, especially when I held her, and, as we relearned how to feed her, the feedings became less of a struggle for her and for us. She exuded warmth and love. Elizabeth, at 18 months old, was a glorious challenge on her own, running here and there and getting into mischief. She was a persistent child who wanted what she wanted. Due to my aggressive bent, I found her persistence an asset. Vicki had some trouble dealing with aggression. The pair of them kept us busy through the day and much of the night. At the same time, I continued to try to put out fires at Willowbrook and at Gouverneur, as staff coverage was an endless struggle. In addition, I was working hard and attending to my clients' needs and cases. With so much time expended with caring for Lara, raising Elizabeth, and the daily interruptions regarding the institutions, it was difficult to even maintain my existing clients, and I needed to do more than that. I needed to grow my practice, to make more money, to make sure Lara would be cared for after I was gone.

Lara seemed to be happy at home but providing 24-hour care was overwhelmingly difficult. I would come home from work to find Vicki exhausted from taking care of the two of them all day. The diapering and, in Lara's case, the long, long feeding. The challenge of caring for Lara was tremendous and literally endless. We knew Elizabeth would learn to use the toilet and feed herself, Lara never would.

Elizabeth was sweet and attentive to Lara, frequently checking her face and head and touching and kissing her. It was so beautiful that I felt I would explode with joy. But an 18 month old is not a caretaker. Without daily assistance, our life was restricted to a commitment to care for Lara 24 hours a day, 365 days a year, forever.

We needed help.

Almost descending from heaven arrived Mrs. Anna Bean. Mrs. Bean was a tiny, elderly woman, the mother of friends of friends of ours from the neighborhood. While visiting our home, they learned that we were looking for someone to help us take care of Lara. Mrs. Bean instantly fell in love with Lara.

"I'll take the job," she said.

Vicki and I looked at each other. I said, "Excuse me?"

"Nanny. Caretaker. For Lara. I'll start tomorrow."

We were concerned whether she could handle it. Mrs. Bean seemed to be not much taller than Lara and she was not a young woman. Her grandchildren were adults.

"Mom can do it," her daughter said.

So Mrs. Bean took care of Lara six days a week, taking Sundays off. And it worked out fine. Everybody was happy. It was a home run.

It was a home run for us but the 5,700 inhabitants of Willowbrook did not fare as well. They did not get a reprieve.

The parents of Alan, a young man in his 20s, retained me to secure damages for injuries sustained in Willowbrook. Alan was severely retarded but was ambulatory and spoke perhaps 20 words. He was beaten so badly by another resident that he sustained a brain concussion and lost his prior ability to speak. Both the testimony of his parents and Alan's records maintained by Willowbrook confirmed that he had the ability to speak about 20 words. Despite their own records and the parent's testimony, the attorney general representing Willowbrook insisted that the employees swore that Alan possessed no speech.

The State called a direct care provider who testified that he cared for Alan on a daily basis for several years and that Alan never spoke. On my cross examination of the witness, the following was elicited:

Q. Did you ever speak with Alan?
A. Yes, on a daily basis.
Q. Did he ever respond to you with words?
A. Never.
Q. Did you ever speak to him other than to give him instructions?

A. No. I only spoke with him to tell him what
to do.

Q. Did he follow your instructions?

A. Always.

Q. Did you ever ask him of anything that
sought or required a verbal answer?

A. Never.

The telling part about this testimony is that neither the
caregiver, nor the attorney representing Willowbrook, ever
considered that asking a mentally retarded person a
question that would invite a verbal response was part of the
job. It says so much about the quality of care and
interaction. Prior to his assault Alan possessed a small
vocabulary that his caregivers never noticed because they
never tried to get him to speak.

Another day while I was visiting at Willowbrook, I
met the Rabbi employed at Willowbrook to serve and assist
the residents living there. Although, the administration was
made wary, defensive and nervous due to the almost daily
influx of media reporters, the Rabbi readily spoke with me.
I asked him to assist me in securing needed and appropriate
chairs and sofas for the wards.

"Too many residents are lying on the floor because
there aren't enough chairs or sofas in the wards," I began.

"Sure, but I could show you a building full of broken
chairs," he responded

"What?" Are you kidding me, is it their fault that they
have nothing to sit on?"

His point was total nonsense. If the chairs were broken, it was the State's job to repair or replace them.

"I could show you thousands of broken mentally retarded *people* residing in the buildings, people you are supposed to support and protect. Shouldn't their personal welfare be your first concern?" I continued.

The conversation ended. He turned and left and thereafter avoided me. Lesson learned? Living or working in an institution twists, anaesthetizes and warps everyone.

Curious that there was no money for chairs but there was money for a paid Rabbi on staff. Such progress!

I knew that individual lawsuits on behalf of individual wrongs could never change the general conditions at Willowbrook or, for that matter, change the way mentally disabled people were viewed and treated. What was needed was an action on behalf of all the residents, what's commonly called a "class action." Despite the fact that Jerry Weingold, the Executive Director of the New York State Association for Retarded Children (NYSARC) had dismissed the idea of a class action suit, I thought such an action was the only way to engineer real and fundamental reform. Realistically, I knew that I could not handle that alone and maintain a law practice to support my family.

It turned out the New York Civil Liberties Union had the same idea. They initiated the new Willowbrook Class Action suit and engaged Bruce Ennis, Esq., as lead counsel. Bruce had previously been involved in the successful class action filed in the State of Alabama (Wyatt v. Stickney). The judge there found conditions at the Partlow State

School to be grossly substandard. He ruled that the mentally retarded residents of the school had a constitutional right to adequate habilitation and directed minimal standards of care and training. This became the basis for the filing of the Willowbrook Class Action.

"We'd like you to participate," Bruce Ennis stated.

"Great!" I said.

"As plaintiff. On behalf of your daughter."

"Oh."

I pointed out that I had removed Lara from Willowbrook.

"Did you have her formally discharged?"

"No. I just scooped her up. I refused to discharge her."

A real school or hospital wouldn't have let me do that.

"Good."

I decided not to have her discharged. Lara had done her time at Willowbrook but it was important to me that she continued to be a part of the Willowbrook battle. She remained a member of the Willowbrook Class Action. Although she would never know it, it was her fight.

I prepared a statement of the facts and circumstances relating to the claim on behalf of Lara for the Civil Liberties Union. I swore to the following:

> At the time my daughter was admitted to Willowbrook she had been hospitalized on several occasions due to seizures and complications stemming from her brain injury requiring continuous medical surveillance which resulted in her admission as an emergency case.

Before my daughter was one (1) year of age she was diagnosed as being profoundly retarded with multiple physical disabilities rendering her totally unable to care for even her most simple and basic needs. My wife and I desired to keep our daughter at home with us and contacted the Department of Mental Hygiene for assistance with a program.

We were advised that no programs existed for our daughter while she lived at home, that her condition was hopeless and she should be institutionalized. Further, if she could be admitted to Willowbrook, a program was available for her in the Infant Therapy Center there, and that, after all, was her only hope for any habilitation program. If we kept her at home we would be on our own to locate non-existent programs. As a final argument in favor of immediate institutionalization at Willowbrook we were warned of the waiting list of anywhere from twelve (12) to twenty-four (24) months at that time which would expand to six (6) years or longer once she reached the age of six (6) to eight (8) years of age. Once she was that age, we were told, as a practical matter, her chances for admission to a State school for the retarded were nil. In addition, we were reminded that we must concern ourselves with the problem our daughter would face upon our death if she were kept at home.

Faced with all of the above which made us feel helpless in our desire to keep our daughter at home and guilty at the thought of denying her the 'opportunity' for early institutionalization, we were compelled to prepare and process in April, 1969, an application for emergency admission of our daughter to Willowbrook. Shortly after she became fourteen (14) months of age, and on July 31,1969, my wife and I painfully, sorrowfully, guiltily and under absolute compulsion, 'voluntarily' delivered our daughter, Lara, to Building 14 at the Willowbrook State School. The feelings of helplessness, hopelessness, bitterness, emptiness, timidity, fear, pain, guilt and compulsion of this absolutely involuntary act, shall never be forgotten by me for as long as I live.

I went on to reiterate that the job freeze throughout the State, which began in December 1970, decimated the already overworked staff at Willowbrook. Children began to die as a direct result of the inability of the staff to properly feed and care for the residents. Specifically, Dr. Hammond had admitted to the parents and others at a meeting of the Board of Visitors "that children had died as a direct result of a critical staff shortage, children would continue to die, the deaths were primarily among the youngest most frail residents and that he was powerless to prevent such further deaths..."

Lara was among "the youngest most frail residents" he was speaking about. We discussed the list of named plaintiffs. And then they commenced the Class Action without my direct participation, which suited me fine.

I liked people. I liked the New York Civil Liberties Union. And I liked their mission. What I did not like was working by committee. I worked better alone.

Just the same, I was glad to be at a few of the meetings Bruce Ennis invited me to attend. I was glad that I was invited to be a named plaintiff on Lara's behalf, in the Class Action. The Willowbrook Class Action would seek the closing of Willowbrook State School and the placement of its residents into small community residences.

Unfortunately, many of the voluntary agencies operating community residences or "hostels" accepted only high functioning mentally retarded individuals. I guess they were unable to accept the view that all mentally retarded people were capable of residing in something called a "home." The goal for the class action suit was to foster a view that all mentally retarded people, irrespective of the degree of their disability, deserved and were capable of living in a "home," a "community residence" or "group home."

Personally I loathed the term "hostel" applied to community residences. It was the same as using the term "state school" for an institution, or "exodus" for programs to shuffle mentally retarded people from institution to institution, or speaking of "decompression" when applied to relieving the gross overcrowding at Willowbrook. All of these terms were diversions from reality, attempts to camouflage the truth. Unfortunately, some of the voluntary agencies fell into the same game of charades by displaying placards imploring, "DON'T BE HOSTILE TO HOSTELS." Give me a break, call them "homes" – dummy!

I sought small homes or apartments, accommodating a maximum of three residents. This seemed to be the only way to make sure mentally retarded people lived in regular homes and got adequate care and supervision.

The goal of a three resident maximum was based upon my personal observations and conclusions and was confirmed by medical and mental retardation experts I had read and consulted with. It was obvious that the more capable individuals had the resources and ability to function well in larger groups of people. Conversely, the less capable the individual the more difficult it became to interact with a large group. The more retarded the person, the smaller the group needed be. I urged that the profoundly retarded reside in homes limited three residents and the staff necessary to care for them. Given this increasingly accepted expert opinion, it seemed to defy logic that large institutions were used to house the most profoundly retarded. If one were to design a system guaranteed to fail the most needy, it would be hard to come up with one more suited to failure than Willowbrook, with its 5,700 residents. It became my mission to champion three-bed homes for the profoundly and severely mentally retarded.

Until appropriate community placements could be effected, conditions at Willowbrook, especially hiring and maintaining trained staff in adequate numbers, had to be addressed and corrected. Those conditions included all programming (education, rehabilitation, habilitation and therapies); toilet training; environment; developmental plans for each resident; the termination of abuse such as restraints, labor, aversive techniques and behavior modification; research and medication; and the provision of living arrangements that would afford the residents privacy, dignity, comfort and sanitation. And decent, functioning bathrooms. Who doesn't deserve a decent bathroom?

On March 17, 1972, the New York Civil Liberties Union and the Legal Aid Society filed separate complaints in the Willowbrook Class Action in the United States District Court in Brooklyn, New York on behalf of the residents living in the Willowbrook State School, located on Victory Boulevard, Staten Island, New York. The case was assigned to Judge Orrin G. Judd of the United States District Court, Eastern District of New York.

At the time of the filing, Willowbrook operated 43 buildings, housing 5,700 residents. The institution was 65% over capacity (the actual capacity being but 3,700 residents) and more than 75% of the residents were severely or profoundly retarded. On top of the dangerous overcrowding, it is safe to say the facility was tragically, fatally understaffed.

When the Class Action was filed it became clear that the State would not roll over. Led by the Attorney General Louis Lefkowitz, nothing was going to be easy. Unlike the officials in Alabama in the Wyatt case, who acknowledged that Partlow State School was a miserable place, New York State refused to consent to anything. Any victory secured would be earned with blood. Bruce Ennis pressed for relief from the horrific conditions existing at Willowbrook, especially following the funding slashes. He secured several preliminary orders requiring better staff coverage but Willowbrook continued to be a snake pit, the staff numbers stayed low and the resident numbers stayed high. Bruce had to engage in heated battles to get the State to disclose basic documents and to secure simple admissions. It took countless oral depositions to get any information that was sworn and reliable.

After three years of hand-to-hand combat between attorneys for the Civil Liberties Union and Legal Aid Society and those for the New York State Attorney General, numerous hearings, motions, depositions, and testimony from witnesses and experts and reams and reams of pages of records and papers, the State finally realized the ramifications of the horrific truths which had been revealed. They could not win. The State elected to end the battle, settle, and sidestep the embarrassment of a full trial. No longer was the State willing to sustain a cascade of public relations disasters. The trial would be a display of the worst the State had to offer.

The State was not really embarrassed. This was politics, the normal give-and-take resulting in the fewest real changes. It simply pretended to concede.

11

MORE CUTS

In 1974, they renamed Willowbrook the Staten Island Developmental Center but the name did not stick. Willowbrook was Willowbrook. As Malachy McCourt liked to tell me, "Ye can call shit 'roses,' but I wouldn't put it in a vase She was safe and well but was still living far from us and received little, if any, therapeutic services, although she was being held, touched and spoken to. This was a better situation but still far short of our goal.

In an effort to quell the opposition by parents, the State named Dr. Lawrence C. Kolb to be the new Commissioner of the Department of Mental Hygiene in January 1975. Dr. Kolb replaced Dr. Alan Miller, whom I had knocked heads with regarding the closings of Gouverneur and Sampson.

A blanket of snow coated the lawn in front of our building that made the apartment house feel cozier. Vicki played with Elizabeth while I sat on the couch, writing on a legal pad.

"What do you know about Dr. Kolb?" Vicki asked.

"He's a psychiatrist."

"Okay. What about his experience with the mentally retarded?"

"None, as far as I know. And little if any as an administrator.

"So what are you working on?"

"A letter to the New York Times. Want to read it?" She took my place on the couch and I took hers on the carpet. Elizabeth immediately jumped on me, it being such a rarity for daddy to be both home and not working. And I was in heaven. I thought, why am I always working when all I want to do is lie on a carpet with my kids climbing on me?

The letter stated:

> The State of New York has once again closed its eyes and turned its back on reality and honesty in its futile effort to stem the tide of critical analysis of its relentless mistreatment and disregard of the rights of its mentally retarded.
>
> This time, under the alleged new administration of Gov. Carey, it is business as usual as far as the Department of Mental Hygiene is concerned.
>
> The appointment of Dr. Lawrence C. Kolb as the new Commissioner of the Department of Mental Hygiene removes the stench of the previous administration, but replaces it with a person who, at best, lacks the necessary knowledge and sensitivity

in the field of mental retardation and the system of institutionalization.

In Dr. Kolb's press conference following his swearing in ceremony as Commissioner, he proved that he was absolutely unqualified for the job he had just accepted. His own words serve as a forceful condemnation and must serve as the epitaph for his Commissionership. The Department of Mental Hygiene and the new administration were so proud of their press conference that the questions and answers were set out at length on page 3 of the January 17, 1975 issue of the publication of the Department of Mental Hygiene entitled "Mental Hygiene News."

After making numerous references to institutionalized people as being "seriously brain-damaged", "seriously disturbed" and "profoundly brain-damaged" and then taking a backhanded slap at the families of these handicapped persons, he concludes with a most shocking avowal of his new and enlightened policy, to wit: "The real mental health effort must be taken with those who can be maintained and who will become active members in our communities."

Are we again to be saddled with a Commissioner devoted to institutions with back wards, where the profoundly retarded are offered only secrecy and stagnation, and offering only a real effort for those who can pass for normal?

We can not afford a Commissioner lacking in knowledge, lacking awareness and lacking in imagination, who is willing, at this late date, to accept as his own policies, the long standing policies of his many predecessors, which have proven to be erroneous and horrifyingly destructive, to those it is allegedly designed to help.

The New York Times did not print my letter.

In the later part of April 1975, about a week before the scheduled execution of the Consent Judgment on April 30th, I was at my office working on a case. I got a call from Tony Pinto.

"The Department of Mental Hygiene is getting its budget cut."

"By how much?"

"What I heard was several million dollars."

Considering how under budgeted and understaffed Willowbrook and similar state institutions already were, those cuts would be devastating. Worse, we knew the judgment ending the class action was coming up shortly, that the Judge would order changes and that those changes would cost money to implement.

I telephoned Bruce Ennis at the New York Civil Liberties Union and gave him the rundown.

"Forget it," he said.

"What do you mean 'Forget it'?"

"It's too late."

It reminded me of what Dr. Hammond said when Gouverneur was being closed: Nothing could alter, amend or cancel the decision. I concluded that Bruce had been involved with the project long enough and was ready to move on to the next project.

Fair enough, Bruce and the Civil Liberties Union had commenced the Willowbrook Class Action and waged a long battle. I would never stand in their way. I would only step up if, as in this case, they were apparently through.

"Okay, Bruce," I said. "Unless the Commissioner agrees in writing before Judge Judd that there will be no budget cuts for the Department of Mental Hygiene, I will oppose the execution of the Consent Judgment."

I could hear him gasp. "What?"

"The parents will support me."

"But, but…what we've worked for—"

"Is useless without money to implement it."

"*Murray…*"

Everybody thinks my name is going to calm me. I was perfectly calm.

Bruce was not. He let loose a few harsh words and hung up. But he called back later.

"You got what you wanted. The State agrees to maintain the budget for the mentally retarded without any cuts. Happy?"

"I will be. When the Commissioner confirms that in writing, on the record, in front of the judge."

"Deputy Commissioner Robert Hayes will appear before the Court and submit his confirmation, together with a written statement to be placed on the record, assuring that the budget for the mentally retarded was not and will not be cut! *Happy?*"

We should all be happy. On April 30, 1975, all attorneys, many plaintiffs and defendants, including Deputy Commissioner Robert Hayes, appeared before Judge Judd. After Bob Hayes delivered Commissioner Kolb's letter to the Court agreeing that the budget for the mentally retarded would not be reduced or cut, all parties signed the Willowbrook Consent Judgment. Judge Judd formally executed the Final Judgment that day. Several days later on May 5, 1975, the Willowbrook Consent Judgment was entered by the Clerk.

The Willowbrook Consent Judgment contained a lengthy Appendix "A" of Steps, Standards and Procedures set forth on 29 single-spaced pages covering 23 topics. Naturally, we made some mistakes.

There are two mistakes that I acknowledge and continue to regret. My first was failing to press harder and further to secure compliance with the provisions in the Willowbrook Consent Judgment with all due speed. A time constraint was necessary because the State would always delay, delay, delay. That was their practice. We won an extraordinary victory but the public's attention span is short. The world moves quickly and focus seems to flit from disaster to disaster.

My second mistake relates to Paragraph 2 of the Final Judgment, which provides:

Within their lawful authority, including the State constitution and applicable State laws, *and subject to any legislative approval that may be required,* defendants are hereby ordered and enjoined to take all actions necessary to secure implementation of the steps, standards and procedures contained in this judgment and in Appendix "A" hereto... [emphasis added]

"Bruce!" I insisted "Can't you see what this wording allows? The Legislature could just refuse to fund the Willowbrook Consent Judgment. And if they do, the defendants are off the hook. The provision must be completely eliminated or, alternatively, there must be a provision that the Governor, the commissioners, the State is legally required to implement the Judgment, irrespective of funding!"

Bruce was having no part of it. "No more changes. The deal is done." I could have pressed the point, gone straight to the parents the way I did with other issues or gone straight to the press or gone before Judge Judd. Instead, we had a situation where, if the State did not like the way the Willowbrook Review Panel was operating, they could just convince the legislature to cut off our funding.

According to Bruce, that could just never happen. Regrettably, I failed to press the issue.

PART TWO

12

WHY CAN'T LARA TALK?

Vicki and I were living in Bayside, Queens with Elizabeth, who had become a feisty, smart, beautiful and persistent five year-old. Elizabeth was a magnificent handful for Vicki and me. She questioned everything and pressed for a sensible answer. Elizabeth would confront us, face-to-face, nose to nose. Vicki was not used to dealing with such confrontations and challenges but that stuff was right in my wheelhouse. Elizabeth wanted to know what was wrong with Lara and was growing tired of the answer: "Because she was born that way." She continued to push and demand more.

I had just dropped off Vicki for a family visit, while Elizabeth and I went to pick up Lara for a weekend visit. As Vicki got out of the car and shut the door, Elizabeth again demanded, "Why can't Lara talk?"

"I've told you why, many times" I said. The answer was incomplete and she knew it.

I looked in the rear view mirror and I could see her buckled into her child seat, little arms folded and jaw fixed. She was not going to settle for the same old platitude.

"Are you angry?" I asked.

Tight lipped, she nodded.

"Are you unhappy with my answer?"

Again she nodded.

"Do you want to know more?"

She again nodded yes and loosened her lips and arms.

"Okay, sweetheart. I told you the truth, part of Lara's problems happened before she was born but other problems happened just after she was born."

I turned around and swung one arm over the seat, wondering if saying what I was about to say made me a great dad or a lousy one.

"When Lara was born, she had a breathing problem. She couldn't breathe for a long time, so long that it hurt her brain. Breathing and having air is very important for everyone, especially a newborn baby. If a baby does not get air it can hurt the baby's brain. The doctors tried to help Lara but by the time she got enough air, her brain was hurt. This won't happen to you. You're a big healthy girl and you breathe just fine." She considered what I had said, nodded, and never asked again.

Eventually, Anna Bean, Lara's elderly nanny, ran out of gas and we were unable to replace her with someone capable and willing to care for her. Through some divine intervention, we were able to secure a spot for Lara in a specialized Tay-Sachs Unit in the Brooklyn Chronic

Hospital. Tay-Sachs disease is a recessive genetic disorder found in Ashkenazi Jews and Cajuns from southern Louisiana. Tay-Sachs patients often have symptoms similar to Lara's in that they are profoundly retarded and require complete 24/7 care. Unlike Lara, they have a very abbreviated life span, just a few years, at most. All the children in that Unit, including Lara, were handled as if they were rare jewels. There was no therapy provided but Lara received magnificent physical care and attention. She was safe. We visited her regularly and brought her home most weekends. Despite the wonderful care, it was difficult visiting a unit where all the other children were not expected to live beyond their first or second birthday. And we knew that Lara could not stay indefinitely, her condition was not considered terminal.

13

WILLOWBROOK REVIEW PANEL

When the Class Action resulted in the entry of the Willowbrook Consent Judgment, with its lengthy Appendix "A" of Steps, Standards and Procedures, the judge declared that it was "to be enforced by a newly created Review Panel of seven individuals, three to be named by the plaintiffs, two to be named by the defendants, and two experts were to be agreed upon by the parties." In the summer of 1975, when the Review Panel was organized, I was 37 years old. I was busy with my own practice and other handicap cases but I knew I had to make time for the Panel.

The plaintiffs designated Michael Lottman, Linda Glenn and me, as Panel members, and named Dr. James Clements, as one of the experts. Although the Consent Judgment provided that the experts were to be jointly selected by both sides, the attorneys agreed that each side would select one expert. Bruce Ennis did not think that the State would approve of Linda Glenn as an expert. She was viewed as an ideologue. So, we named her a plaintiffs' panel member. However, the State liked Jim Clements. Even though he was on our side, his soft southern drawl could lull them to sleep. We named him our expert.

The defendants, the State, chose Dr. William Bitner and Dr. Samuel Ornstein as their representatives, and they named David Rosen as the other expert. We met at an office made available to us in the World Trade Center in lower Manhattan.

In spite of the fact that I would be a part of a committee and required to work in a panel of seven people, I was anxious to get started. I believed they could never co-opt me but felt I needed a backup plan.

I telephoned Malachy.

"Malachy, I've been designated to be a member of the Review Panel."

"Of course, Muddy. You were destined to be the one of first people chosen. Everyone expected that," he said in his rolling brogue. His brogue shaved the r's into d's and Murray became "Muddy." But not when he referred to me as "my son," something he seemed unaware of. "You're knowledgeable, bright and articulate, it was only a matter of time before your skills were recognized."

"Listen, Malachy. I need you to check on me and immediately let me know if I become a bureaucrat or forget my obligations to Lara and the Willowbrook Class."

"No problem my dear friend. If you blow up like a balloon, ye want me to stick a pin in you."

"Something like that."

"This is an easy job. I'll have nothing to do."

A few days later, I received a telephone call from the office of Dr. Samuel Ornstein—one of the State's representatives— to inform me of the time and place of the first *official* meeting of the Panel. Dr. Ornstein was an Assistant Commissioner of the Department of Mental Hygiene, Bureau of Mental Retardation. I told his secretary to inform Dr. Ornstein that I was anxious to review some specific documents and asked that he bring those documents to the meeting. Within five minutes of that conversation, his office called back to inform me that Dr. Ornstein "felt that it was not necessary for him to bring the documents because the documents to be provided will be determined by the members at the meeting."

"Tell Dr. Ornstein that I am a member of the Review Panel. I want to review the documents I asked for at the meeting and I do not care whether anyone else wants to review them. No one will tell me what documents I may or may not see," I seethed.

The meeting was called to order.

Jim Clements was a six-foot tall, slim, blond and soft-spoken southern gentleman. He was a pediatrician and had earned a national reputation for his work for providing services to the mentally retarded. He had been the superintendent of the well known and highly regarded Georgia Retardation Center, located in Athens, and simultaneously served as the Planning Director for mental retardation services for the State of Georgia. He was a nationally acclaimed expert in the field. Jim left the state positions to work as a mental retardation expert, addressing the inhumane archaic institutions and focusing on the development of community residential services and community services. Jim was more than a decade older than me and had been in the fray a lot longer.

Linda Glenn was a short, slim, pretty young woman with light brown hair. Her lack of make-up and conservative dress belied how pretty she was. She was about 30 years old but was able to speak to retarded people, young or old, with the calm and truly engaged demeanor. She was an "old soul" and possessed a loving grace that drew people to her. I envied her noted expertise in the theory of normalization and the services for and treatment of the mentally retarded. Linda was from Nebraska, a place in the forefront of normalization and community services for the mentally retarded. She also worked with the renowned developer of "normalization," Wolf Wolfensberger at Syracuse University. The principle of normalization strives to provide disabled people with the daily living styles in housing, schooling, employment, exercise, recreation and freedom of choices that would be as close as possible to those available to so-called "normal" people.

Mike Lottman was a few years younger than me, about 5'10" with an average build, dark hair and wore dark eyeglass frames. He became involved in the Willowbrook Class Action as a litigating attorney working for the United States Justice Department as amicus curiae. He was a tough, great lawyer with remarkable writing skills. He was a legal scholar. I was a legal gladiator.

Jim said, "I nominate Murray Schneps as Chairman."

I said, "I respectfully decline." Heads turned. Jim grabbed me by the arm and pulled me out into the hall.

"What's the matter with you? You want to make a difference. Here's your chance!"

"The Chairman is supposed to be an even-handed, objective arbiter, right?"

"So?"

"Do I look objective to you?"

He stared me down, walked back into the room. "I open the floor to other nominations."

Mike said, "I nominate Jim Clements as Chairman."

A quick second. Unanimous. Jim said, "I nominate Murray Schneps as Vice Chairman. There should be no dispute."

There was none. A quick second. Unanimous.

At the meeting, Dr. Ornstein appeared with the documents I had requested and, other than introducing himself, did not speak. Within a few days, James Forde, a Regional Director for the Department of Mental Hygiene, replaced Dr. Ornstein as a defendants' panel member. Jim Forde was a very good man and so was Bill Bitner. Bill was an Associate Commissioner for the New York State Department of Education. Dave Rosen, from the State of Michigan, was the state-nominated expert specializing in the development of community residences.

The members of the plaintiffs' contingent were the only ideologues in the room but that was the easy part. Now we had to learn how quickly we could move a huge bureaucracy into full compliance with all of the terms, conditions and provisions of the lengthy and detailed Consent Judgment. At that point, we did not know whether any of the defendants' designated Panel members would vote with the plaintiffs. Further, it was still an open question as to whether Bill Bitner or Jim Forde would seek to sabotage our efforts or attempt to delay implementation. I gathered, from what Bruce told me about Jim, Linda and Mike, that they were in sync with me. I hoped so. Time would tell.

The purpose of the panel seemed straightforward to me. The Final Judgment, agreed to by all parties, provided:

> Defendants are hereby ordered and enjoined to take all necessary action to secure implementation of the steps, standards and procedures containing in this judgment and in Appendix "A" hereto, which appendix is expressly made part hereof, in a prompt and orderly manner.

This meant that the defendants had the sole obligation to promptly do everything that the Judgment ordered. Period. It was the responsibility of the Willowbrook Review Panel to see to it that the defendants did their job. And I was committed to make sure that the defendants would do it "with all due speed" and "in a prompt and orderly manner." To me, yesterday was not soon enough.

The Panel was ordered to "make recommendations to the defendants of steps deemed necessary to achieve or maintain compliance with this judgment." In addition, the

Willowbrook Review Panel was to make informal suggestions to the defendants, "which in their opinion will facilitate compliance with the judgment." For the most part, we opted for formal recommendations.

Jim, Mike, Linda and I were not chosen based upon our ability or propensity to compromise. The time for compromising had passed. Now, it was the time for enforcement. We were not diplomats. We were zealous advocates. That was our promise to the parents and to the residents at Willowbrook. And it was my promise to Lara. In the very first formal recommendation issued by the Willowbrook Review Panel, our heels were dug in deeply and firmly. We were taking a tough and aggressive position. This should have been a wake-up call to the defendants that we meant business. They got the message and delay, delay, delay was their first line of defense.

What was wrong with requiring the State to comply with its own agreement? After all, the Willowbrook Consent Judgment was not solely the plaintiffs' judgment, it was also the defendants' judgment. And what was wrong with refusing to make any compromise that altered the Court's Final Judgment? A *consent* judgment.

Both the plaintiffs and the defendants had the right, even the obligation on the part of the plaintiffs, to name ideologues on their own side. The plaintiffs wisely did so. The defendants did not initially select obvious ideologues. Certainly, their respective Commissioners and the Governor supervised Bill Bitner and Jim Forde, but they were not ideologues. Ultimately, the State did yell "help" and appointed someone who would pursue and vote positions responsive to the Commissioner and, particularly, the Governor.

The Panel was funded with an annual budget of approximately $300,000. The money covered salaries for our staff, supplies, telephones and a daily fee for the work performed by the panel members. All agreed to in the Consent Judgment.

The Willowbrook Review Panel had offices provided by the State in the World Trade Center. The space was not elaborate but was adequate for our use. Essentially, it was State standard government issue. The offices were furnished with desks, chairs, tables, cabinets, telephones and office supplies. We had an administrative assistant and two secretaries. The offices had an entry/waiting room, a few smaller offices for our staff, plus a multipurpose room with a large conference table and chairs, used also for various meetings. The multipurpose room could accommodate approximately 20 people. During the monthly meetings held in various hotels and State facilities, we met with many State administrators and representatives of voluntary agencies to discuss our findings, their plans and complaints, and our thinking.

The Panel held regular meetings one weekend a month. Since my law office was several blocks away from the World Trade Center, I could walk there and I went to the office on a regular basis during the week and spoke with our Executive Director, Jennifer L. Howse, Ph.D., almost daily. I spoke to Jim Clements and Mike Lottman on a regular basis. I spoke with Linda Glenn less frequently. I spoke with Bill Bitner, David Rosen, and Jim Forde as needed. We all got along very well together and respected each other.

Critics and skeptics marveled at the odds against our success. In truth, the triumph of Bruce Ennis and his team at the New York Civil Liberties Union (NYCLU) was tremendous. But ultimately, Bruce took a bow and exited, leaving us to assure that the hard-won changes were actually implemented.

14

THE PRESS

Time was our enemy. First, the residents were stuck in Willowbrook until we could place them in the community. And residents stuck in Willowbrook too long had a tendency to deteriorate and die. Second, community conscience flits to the latest outrage. For the moment—from the time Geraldo Rivera took on this issue—we were news. I mean real news. The Vietnam War was being waged and that was the most important news in print and on air. And yet, Geraldo Rivera and ABC News covered our story on an almost daily basis. While the Vietnam story got 20 minutes coverage on its show, we got 10 to 15 minutes coverage as well. It was a fantastic boon to us and I will always appreciate Geraldo and his boss, Al Primo, who permitted the story to run daily as it progressed, long after other TV stations walked away. The fact that TV audiences were watching had to affect our success in court. And now, with the courtroom drama over, I knew audiences would move on. We would lose public support to the next crisis.

And talking to cameras was a skill. I was called to Willowbrook many times to talk to the press. I knew what was important to say. I had spoken in public forums, and during visits by legislators at Willowbrook. I could present statements in different sound bites: 30 seconds, one minute, two minutes, five minutes, 30 minutes, etc. They stood me before the camera, gave me a cue, and I made my statement.

The very first time I had been interviewed on TV I came away pretty happy with the results. I thought I had been clear, concise and professional. I called Vicki and had her call everyone we knew to tell them I would be on the evening news.

Then I watched them shoot the statement of Assemblyman Andrew Stein. He botched it. He stammered and faltered. His assistant asked the reporter for a retake. His second take was not much better.

I rushed home to see myself on television. Friends and colleagues watched on TV's all around the region. We all waited for my debut.

Only Stein appeared. His statement was not our story. We went unrepresented and my big scene landed on the cutting room floor.

I digested what had happened and I learned my lesson.

I was determined that in the future our message would appear on the news. I made sure to promote our position and not simply be grateful that the television reporters were there and reporting. It was critical that they report *our* story.

When Dr. Hammond was still the Director of Willowbrook, he was interviewed on CBS-TV News. I received a phone call the next day.

"This is Pat Collins from CBS News. Would you meet us at Willowbrook tomorrow for an interview in response to Dr. Hammond's statement."

She was referred to me by one of the Benevolent Society officers. I showed up with half a dozen members of the Benevolent Society. Ms. Collins outlined the questions she was planning to ask.

"How difficult is the job that Dr. Hammond must perform and how great a job is he doing taking care of the residents under the circumstances and budget cutting," was one of the questions she would ask.

"About these questions," I said.

"Yes?"

"You might as well give me the answers you want and I can read that."

Her smile stiffened.

I went on. "These questions favor Hammond's position, but they do not give me a chance to talk about what is actually happening at Willowbrook. Unless you ask me about that, I will not do the interview."

A half-dozen parents cringed so hard they nearly doubled over.

"If you won't answer my questions," she said, her smile devoid of joy, "I'll just interview Dr. Hammond again."

"No you won't," I said. "You did not come all the way to Staten Island with a camera crew to interview the same guy you interviewed yesterday."

One of the parents choked out a request. "Murray, can we talk to you?"

They pulled me aside and we huddled.

"Do it. Do the interview," they urged.

"Hey folks, we are in charge here. This crew is costing the station by the minute. She cannot go back empty-handed."

"Murray!" they pleaded. They felt threatened. I did not.

I said, "Look, we are here to present our position and for no other reason. We will not be manipulated by the press."

I held my position, the parents calmed down, the reporter relented, and the reporter and I were satisfied with the story.

Essentially, I had already learned that most of the parents were fearful and were easily cowed by the State or any authority. They were beaten down by the continued suffering of their handicapped children and did not have the tools, the power, or the internal toughness to do more than comply. They exhibited the same kind of submission we associate with victims of the Holocaust.

But compliance with unreasonable demands, even more compliance than the abuser demands, in the hopes that the abuser will leave you alone, is a futile hope. An abuser is never satisfied. Instead, the abuser quickly identifies the weakness and the demands accelerate to a level beyond all practical reason. The victim of abuse who lacks advocacy skills and is without mental and physical power, does the best he or she can do and usually works alone or joins with weak groups. The victim operating alone rarely can attain success.

I am an attorney trained in critical thinking. As a litigator, I was a very aggressive person blessed with a strong sense of ethics. Money was a facilitator—it paid my rent and fed my kids—but was never my motivator. I was committed to doing the right thing, speaking out against unfairness, and protecting those under attack, physical or otherwise. People like Lara, born with no defenses, no language, and, for all practical purposes, no voice, needed a defender with a loud and assertive voice. I volunteered to take the job. I would not forget. I would not give in. I would hold my position.

Although I wanted Lara and all mentally retarded people to receive the best of everything, always, I knew that the State could not, would not and should not be required to provide the best. The standard of "best" is impossibly high. Therefore, my approach to all demands for the mentally retarded would be based upon the development of an individualized prescription for each person.

I can imagine an opponent asserting, "Murray, you preach Communism! From each according to his abilities, to each according to his needs." I view my position in terms of a specific pharmaceutical response. You would not give everyone insulin. It would be murderous. But you would not deny insulin to someone who needed it. That would be murderous, too.

So my "prescription" plan is designed without considering the issue of cost. When determining what each child requires, it would be unconscionable to offer services at a level lower than the prescription; the Court must order what is required. The issue of that which is the "best" or "excellent" is irrelevant. My goal was to raise the issue and advocate for all services that are "necessary and appropriate" for each person, normal or handicapped. Certainly, everyone must be entitled to all that is required. Who could fairly and reasonably argue against a person receiving what he actually requires?

Now, if only I could get the rest of the world to think that way.

15

COMMUNITY PLACEMENT

At home, Vicki and I were frustrated by our inability to conceive our third child. We sought the best medical help available but got no answers. I can only imagine the pain of people struggling to have a *first* child. We had already been blessed twice. Our Lara was still living at the Richmond Children Center and was safe and well cared for. We brought her home most weekends or visited her at the facility during the week.

And the work with the Panel progressed. I made a conscious decision not to make any permanent personal alliances with any of the Panel members. This way I could remain independent and free to take any proper action or make any statement necessary under the circumstances. I had not entered a popularity contest. I was not there to make friends. Other than my admiration for Bill Bitner, allying with the defendants' selected members was impossible.

Jim Forde, a Regional Director for the Department of Mental Hygiene, had replaced the State's member, Dr. Ornstein. Jim was then replaced by Clarence Sundram, an

Assistant Counsel to the Governor, introducing another level of politics to the panel as he attempted to soften, or to delay, many of our efforts to implement the Consent Judgment. Clarence was bright and never to be considered lightly.

"Murray," Clarence said, in honeyed tones, "you're an attorney, like me. Attorneys always ask for more than they hope for, more than they expect, more than they even want."

"Clarence," I sang back, "this isn't a game. I only want what I asked for and I expect to get it. And what I want is full implementation of the Willowbrook Consent Judgment. Nothing more, nothing less."

Technically, I had alliances with Jim Clements, Mike Lottman and Linda Glenn, but I watched them like a hawk. Hopefully, they also watched me. Too many adults and children died in Willowbrook and too many others were on the verge of death. In fact, all who were living in Willowbrook were dying. For life to continue to thrive, it must be nurtured. No one in Willowbrook was nurtured.

The Consent Judgment required that the Panel develop a Community Placement Plan immediately. We did. The plan presented a realistic expectation for the existence of small community residences, and many parents converted themselves into advocates in favor of community placements and in opposition to institutions.

But some of the parents objected. They wrote and called and met with us, stating in clear terms that they did not want Willowbrook closed.

"Just clean it up."

"Fix the living conditions."

They did not like the idea of community placement. Jim, Mike, Linda and I discussed this at length.

"They buy into the State's propaganda."

"*Which* propaganda?"

"That the mentally retarded can't live at home."

"Or anybody's home. Or a group home."

"Right. They can only be maintained in an institution."

"Because institutions work so well."

"And they'll die if they leave."

The lie that retarded people could not live in a regular home and could only live in residential institutions was reinforced with regularity.

"If my child can live in a regular home, my child would live with me at my home," parents were taught to believe.

It sounded to me like those parents were asking for a cleaner, more efficient warehouse. "And safe, and permanent. Whether I live or die, there will be a place for my child to live and eat and sleep and be safe. Who else would provide that?" Of course, the State. But the State was failing miserably.

I met with the father of a mentally retarded child who resided in Willowbrook. The father attended one of the Open Hearings scheduled by the Panel. He stood up to speak, though that was not required.

"Every day I thank G-d for Willowbrook."

"Why's that?" I asked, it being my turn to moderate.

"My kid can't break anything at Willowbrook. There's nothing to break! I bring him home every weekend, from Friday evening to Sunday evening, to be with the family.

But before I bring him home, I lock up everything he can break out of sight: ashtrays, lamps, dishes, plates, everything!" Sadly, the man was testifying that Willowbrook had helped him sentence his child to a sterile environment, where the boy could do no harm. This was a triumph. And every weekend he sentenced his child, his other children, his wife and himself to live in a homemade warehouse; a sterile place to replicate the Willowbrook warehouse. All in the name of assuring that his handicapped child would not hurt him or damage anyone's possessions.

We had higher goals.

At other meetings some parents made curious comments to me. On several occasions people approached me for the first time and told me that, "I thought you would be much older." Those statements did not surprise. However, on two separate occasions a parent, upon meeting me for the first time, stated, "Oh, I thought you would be much taller." Apparently, they expected me to have the body of a heavy weight boxer. I chewed on that for a while.

16

HUMANITARIAN AWARD

One day, in the early work of the Panel, I got a very ornate envelope from the Institutes of Applied Human Dynamics. This was the school in the Bronx that we had decided was not for Lara before sending her to Willowbrook. It looked like an invitation.

"It's an invitation, all right," I said. I had just come home from the office, still in my suit, and I was sorting the mail on the kitchen counter. Elizabeth was hugging me around my neck, which made reading a challenge. Vicki was getting dinner. I said, "Someone's getting a Humanitarian Award."

"Who?" Vicki asked.

I unfolded the second page. "Me."

She turned to me. "It's about time."

The Institutes of Applied Human Dynamics had honored Vicki and Malachy and Diana McCourt the prior year for all their work on behalf of the retarded and, seemingly, forgot about me. Honestly, I felt slighted but never expressed my disappointment. Perhaps it was their plan to name me the next year.

We talked about it through the evening. I was not a humanitarian. I was an angry father. I was only different from any other father because I was a litigator and knew how to fight. And I did not give up easily.

"Do it," Vicki said. "You're not going to pass up an award like that, are you? You'll have an opportunity to talk to a bunch of people who don't really know what's going on."

"Mmm…"

"And you deserve the recognition."

On May 25, 1975, I spoke before a crowd of 250 people. I acknowledged the Founder and Leader of the Institutes of Applied Human Dynamics, Dr. Jack Gootzeit, a true believer and humanitarian. Then, I reminded the audience that, in spite of the fact that the State officials had congratulated each other for their goodness in executing the Willowbrook Consent Judgment, for us "the party is over and we are left with the confetti, balloons and dirty dishes of enforcement."

I was referring to the Willowbrook Review Panel and the active parents.

The Panel was in the position to direct the Department of Mental Hygiene regarding Willowbrook State School, and other institutions and facilities where the various Willowbrook Class members now resided. The Willowbrook Class members were all people who were on the rolls of Willowbrook on March 17, 1972, the date the action was filed.

Lara was a member of the Willowbrook Class as she remained on the rolls of the institution in spite of the fact that we brought her home on February 21, 1972. At that time I intentionally refused to announce that she would never return and insisted that she remain on the rolls of Willowbrook. Lara had to be a part of the struggle. I was deeply engaged and could not turn back. After all, the world was not, as yet, safe for my Lara.

The most important power granted to the Panel was the authority to determine, prepare, and submit Formal Recommendations to the defendants. This required the defendants to respond to and comply with the Formal Recommendations and move toward full implementation of the Willowbrook Consent Judgment. Initially, the Judgment authorized the defendants to reject the recommendation, requiring the Panel to prove to the court that the recommendation was correct and proper. The burden of proof was on us.

This struck me as ridiculous. We had already won the case. We were just trying to implement its ruling. The burden should have been the defendants' obligation to show we were incorrect.

The defendants rejected a recommendation, our first, requiring that all Willowbrook Class Members be moved directly from the institutions to community residences without interim transfers to other institutions. To some degree, the Court felt we were right but premature.

While the Court gave the State some flexibility in permitting interim transfers to other institutions, the Court agreed with our arguments and decided that, thereafter, all Formal Recommendations of the Willowbrook Review Panel, would be deemed *prima facie* (at first look) proper and correct and further determined that the State would be obligated to have the burden of proof by first proving that each Formal Recommendation was improper or incorrect. What this meant was that, if the State objected to a recommendation, it would have the initial burden of proving that the recommendation was improper.

The burden of proof was now to be carried on the State's back.

This was an unusual process. Normally, whoever objects to the acts of the State, must carry the heavy burden.

And so we chipped away against injustice and gave the Panel a considerable amount of power to go head-to-head with the State and to win.

17

TRANSFERS

Lara came home for weekends with our family, so the weekends that I was busy working with the Review Panel I only got to visit with her in the mornings before I left and in the evenings when I returned home. Vicki had double duty those weekends and her parents often pitched in to help.

At the monthly meetings, our expert, Dr. Jim Clements, held an unwavering belief that using interim institutions, the act of transferring the mentally retarded from one institution to another institution before placing them directly into community residences, not only delayed community placement, but was useless and ultimately injurious. Knowing how bureaucracies worked, it did not take much imagination to realize that once a person was transferred to yet another institution, that "transfer" was likely to be permanent.

The terms "placement" and "transfer" are words of art. Placements are the movement of mentally retarded clients into community residential programs. Transfers are the movement of mentally retarded clients into institutions, usually from institution to institution.

Justice delayed was literally justice denied.

Jim believed that community placement was the only place where development could occur. I recognized the logic and practicality of his belief and adopted his position. It became my firm position that all institutions for the mentally retarded should be closed and replaced with three-bed community residential group home and apartments.

At Panel meetings, we would push for eliminating interim placements and pressed for direct transfer from Willowbrook and other institutions to community residences. The sooner we empty Willowbrook and place its residents in the community, the closer we get to our goal of closing all institutions for the mentally retarded. I recall that all of the Panel members voted in favor of this formal recommendation. This recommendation set a tone that the defendants hated. They rejected our formal recommendation and a major battle began.

The defendants brought in their heavy guns. The State dragged in Helen Kaplan, Executive Director of the Nassau County Association for Retarded Children, to testify on the defendants' behalf. I thought of her as a hypocrite for the defense, and I referred to her as Mary Sunshine. At first, her behavior confused me. How could a leader for programs supporting the mentally retarded testify in favor of the State and against the mentally retarded class members of the Willowbrook Consent Judgment? I knew her and it is true that she did a great job as Executive

Director for the Nassau County Association for Retarded Children. But she did not believe in the right, benefit, or need to have severely and profoundly retarded people living in community residences. She believed that multiply handicapped severely and profoundly retarded people should reside in institutions, "good ones" (which she somehow believed to exist) but institutions nonetheless. The terms "good" and "institution" in the same sentence is mutually exclusive. A "good institution" is an oxymoron.

I knew that Helen had not and would not provide services to any multiply handicapped severely or profoundly retarded people. She did not know anything about them. She held the opinion that it was improper and inappropriate for them to be in community residences, as they belonged in institutions. This belief was based on nothing—no research and no experience. It was just her opinion. She operated day care programs, and residential group homes which she and the New York State Association for Retarded Children called "hostels" for mildly and moderately retarded people. Although she claimed that she provided services to severely retarded people, it was my belief that she did not know what a profoundly or severely retarded person was. In fact, she privately admitted to me that she refused to provide services to such individuals.

It was my conclusion that Helen's "belief" that the profoundly and severely retarded belonged in institutions was threefold: (1) she did not want to affect her funding for day care services and homes for the retarded she served; (2)

she was committed to serve the mildly and moderately retarded who stayed home and never resided in Willowbrook or any other institution; and (3) she did not want to provide services to the multiply handicapped profoundly or severely retarded. Her chief supporters were the parents whose children were able to stay home, the children not forced into the institutions.

I felt that she tried to accomplish her goals on the backs of the multiply handicapped and profoundly and severely retarded. If Helen had elected to only serve the mildly and moderately retarded, I would have had no objection and would continue to praise her. However, when she elected to make an active move to minimize severely and profoundly retarded people and, thereby, force them to continue to live in institutions, that was my business. At that point she became an enemy.

Mike Lottman and I acted as attorneys for the Willowbrook Review Panel and handled the legal procedures regarding formal recommendations, with the assistance and participation of Chris Hansen, Esq., of the New York Civil Liberties Union. Mike was a wonderful lawyer. He handled much of the work in drawing of the legal paper work for the Panel. He worked tirelessly. I wrote well and emotionally but Mike wrote like a legal scholar. We worked together smoothly and cooperatively with rarely a disagreement. Chris was an excellent attorney. At first blush, he seemed to be too gentle to be a litigator or an advocate. But rue the day for anyone who underestimated him, as he was a real litigator, a real advocate.

We learned that I would have the responsibility of cross-examining Helen Kaplan. That determination was based upon my request with the happy approval of Mike Lottman and Chris Hansen. The goal of my cross-examination of Helen Kaplan was designed to emphasize the fact that, whatever expertise she had was in the area of day programs and group homes for the mildly and moderately mentally retarded, she had no knowledge or experience in the area of institutions for the mentally retarded, especially providing services to the severely and profoundly multiply handicapped mentally retarded.

"Can you describe the mentally retarded individuals you provide programming and residential services to?" I asked.

"They are mildly and moderately retarded and a few are severely retarded," she answered.

"Do you provide services to severely or profoundly mentally retarded multiply handicapped people?" I pressed.

"No," she replied.

"Have you ever provided programs or residential services to any severely or profoundly mentally retarded multiply handicapped person?" I moved ahead.

"No."

"Would you be willing to provide such services to any of the severely or profoundly mentally retarded multiply handicapped individuals who currently reside in Willowbrook," I demanded.

"No, I would not," she insisted.

"Why not?," I insisted.

She cleared her throat. Twice.

"Is it because you believe that they should be provided all services and residential programs in residential institutions," I charged.

"Yes, but good institutions," she smirked.

"Have you ever managed or provided any services, programming or residential, to any mentally retarded people residing in an institution?"

"No."

There was nothing else to ask her. Any of her testimony in support of institutionalization for the mentally retarded was nullified.

Following that cross-examination, people like Helen Kaplan and her supporters viewed me to be a vicious radical, a nutty ideologue. Malachy assured me, "Muddy, your enemies are not worthy of you." And neither were the enemies of the Willowbrook Review Panel.

18

OTHER BATTLES

Although Lara could not participate in my work, she was the inspiration for all I did. We continued to bring her home for most weekends or visited her at Willowbrook, the Tay Sachs Unit or Richmond Children Center. Her medical condition was stable, without bouts of pneumonia and further hospitalizations.

She was always an important member of our family and, although it was not calculable, it appeared to us that Lara responded to our voices and seemed more relaxed by our touch.

During these years I handled many lawsuits regarding the handicapped. Some cases were downright impossible to win but each sought to make a point. People had to know the truth about the mentally retarded: that they were entitled to equality in life, liberty, opportunity and care. Yet somehow, I was always surprised, amazed, and disappointed when I lost. Once I got into the fray, I thought that I should and would win every case.

I filed an action in the name of my daughter, under *Schneps v. Nyquist*. This case sought to simplify the funding of school services to handicapped children residing in the community for the full 12-month year. The State automatically paid for school costs and tuition for 10 months but required a court order to secure payment for school tuition during the months of July and August. Even though the New York State Education Law defined the school year as 12 months, the case was ultimately lost. No funding streams were created by the State to fund mentally retarded children residing at home or in community residences who required 12- month educational programs. To request funding for July and August a costly separate legal proceeding was necessary. And it was not always successful if not handled properly. With the establishment of community residences, it was necessary to change the thinking of the State legislature to alter their funding processes.

Previously, in *Seitelman v. Lavine,* the New York State Court of Appeals held that a mentally retarded individual residing in the State of New York, who was required to secure residential programs in an out-of-state school in Vineland, New Jersey, because residential treatment was not available for him in New York State, was entitled to receive funding as a New York State domiciliary (domicile is akin to citizenship).

In *Slavin v. Secretary of the Dept. of H.E.W.,* a companion state case with *Seitelman*, the Federal District Court ruled that a New York State mentally retarded resident who required residential programs in Vineland,

New Jersey, was entitled to Federal Supplemental Security Income (SSI) disability payments from New York State rather than from New Jersey, as he was a New York State domiciliary. The New York State supplemental payments were greater than those from New Jersey.

The *Seitelman* and *Slavin* cases settled the funding issue for handicapped people who required out-of-state residential services, allowing them to receive funding from their respective home states.

Not only was I busy filing lawsuits against the State, but the State was busy suing many parents of children living in institutions for reimbursement of the costs for their institutionalization. When the State elected to file suit against Vicki and me for the costs for Lara's attending and residing at Willowbrook, I happily took up the challenge. I sought the dismissal of the case arguing that Willowbrook was not entitled to receive payment because they failed to provide proper care, treatment and supervision to Lara. Just like any business case, if the consumer does not receive what he bought the consumer does not have to pay. The State failed to defend the conditions at Willowbrook, so the appellate court dismissed the State's complaint (*New York State Department of Mental Hygiene v. Schneps*).

I always knew that the State's arrogance would be our strength. The State filed several actions seeking payment from parents with children residing in New York State institutions for the mentally retarded. I am proud to note that only two families secured dismissal of such cases, my case and an action against another parent whose child resided in Willowbrook. I represented that family.

Setting the stage for the battles over group homes was the so-called Padavan Law, also known as the "Site selection of community residential facilities" (Mental Hygiene Law, Section 41.34). New York State Senator Frank Padavan vehemently opposed group homes, especially for the severely and profoundly retarded. He drafted and secured the enactment of the site selection provision for the purpose of preventing the opening of group homes for the mentally retarded in residential communities. Fortunately, Sen. Padavan was an engineer and not a lawyer. Therefore, the statute which he drafted, supported and had enacted, failed to achieve its goal. The language made it wholly unnecessary to attack the statute as being unconstitutional. It provided that any proposed community residential facility "which would result in a concentration" of like facilities so that the "nature and character of the area . . . would be substantially altered," could be barred. Conversely, all others were permissible. Since it is impossible to prove the effect of something that did not yet exist, opponents could never prove that any particular proposed group home would be the tipping point where the "nature and character of the area . . . would be altered." I do not believe that a single community residence for the mentally retarded was rejected or prevented from opening pursuant to Sen. Padavan's site selection law. In fact, the statute he was so proud of worked completely opposite to his intention. Group homes could not be prevented.

In a letter to the New York Times on May 1, 1981, Sen. Padavan, as the Chairman of the New York State Senate Committee on Mental Hygiene, opposed any funding to the Willowbrook Review Panel, encouraged slowing down the pace of opening community residences, and supported others of his ilk in doing the same.

Much later, he tried to take credit for the unintended consequence of his law: the opening of group homes. Perhaps time changed him from an opponent to a supporter but I do not think so. A politician is a politician.

19

NOT ON MY BLOCK

The tony Queens County neighborhood of Little Neck would be the site of our next battle over community housing for retarded people.

Though technically part of New York City, Little Neck sits on the north shore of Long Island, on Long Island Sound, literally a stone's throw from Great Neck, the presumed site of Fitzgerald's *The Great Gatsby*. Fitzgerald lived in Great Neck in the 1920s and was believed to have set the novel there, renaming the town. While Scott and Zelda Fitzgerald's alcoholism and mental illness were tolerated, if not celebrated, half a century later, the notion of a single group home for the mentally retarded was repelled as if mental retardation were contagious.

Some neighbors feared the mentally retarded, the mentally ill, and the handicapped. I am certain they did not know the difference between the mentally retarded and the mentally ill, or care to know. "Not on my block" became their mantra.

The Working Organization for Retarded Children (WORC) was originally a women's organization seeking to raise money to improve the lives of the mentally retarded children living in Willowbrook. The organization grew and the participants realized that parties and candy were not enough. The mentally retarded needed real lives. While the organization continued to visit the institution and work with the residents, it began to raise money for the purpose of finding, purchasing, renovating, and opening group homes for multiply handicapped, profoundly and severely mentally retarded children.

To do that they needed to incorporate and for that they needed a lawyer, and I was it. A lawyer who was committed to the cause and would work cheap. Vicki was a co-founder of WORC, so I was the logical choice.

I helped them incorporate and later helped them open several group homes. And I was on hand when they sought to open the first group home in Gatsby's stomping ground.

WORC began a search for appropriate, available single-family residences in northeast Queens. (To those outside the region: Queens, like Brooklyn, is part of New York City. Less populated than Manhattan but more populated than most suburbs.) WORC held fundraisers, received a grant from Geraldo Rivera's "One to One Charity," and pulled together the assets to buy a lovely home. When Geraldo became involved with Willowbrook he got to know Vicki and me. He aligned himself with our goal to open group homes for severely and profoundly mentally retarded children and to create a facility for Lara.

"One to One" held an all-day outing. It was organized by Geraldo and held in the huge Sheep Meadow of Central Park in New York City for hundreds of mentally retarded people. The key for the outing was that each mentally retarded person was buddied with a specially selected caregiver who stayed with him or her for the entire day of games and fun and food. It was a great success.

The outing was followed by a benefit concert starring John Lennon and Yoko Ono, and other stars like Roberta Flack and Bowser of the rock and roll group Sha Na Na. Proceeds from the concert funded four voluntary agencies, including WORC.

Then WORC found the house we had been looking for on Gaskel Road. It was in serviceable shape, with a yard, access, multiple bathrooms and bedrooms, and sunshine. We executed a contract of purchase. Then, in an act of spectacular good faith, we notified neighbors and local community and governmental agencies of our intention to purchase the house and develop a group home for mentally retarded children. We provided full disclosure and open communication of information and our plans. What is the worst that could happen?

Several neighbors welcomed our plans and some of them became active members of WORC.

"Welcome to the neighborhood!"

"We think it's wonderful what you're doing!"

"How can we help?"

I worried the influx of new WORC members would take over the agency and undermine our goals. This would have been a real problem, if it had happened. We need not have worried about too many new supporters. Instead, the opponents of the group home conducted their own membership drive to take over an existing community group, the Little Neck Community Association.

Once they did that, I realized we were facing a lawsuit by a committed organization, energized by fear and prejudice. Since I was already WORC's attorney, they made me the spokesperson and let me handle the opponents.

Several supporters held open meetings in their homes. I thought this showed a high level of commitment and personal integrity. It takes a lot to serve coffee and cake on your nice china with the knowledge that, at any moment, a fistfight might break out. We laid out our arguments about why institutions do not work and why small group homes do. Some neighbors liked what we had to say. Some neighbors did not like what we had to say but understood that the mentally retarded had the right to live anywhere. And some neighbors hated what we were planning to do. Their self-interest and bigotry overwhelmed them and they hardened their opposition.

At one home meeting a tall and balding stockbroker engaged me in a battle of words over whether it was even appropriate to have severely and profoundly retarded children living in his community. Our discussion went on for more than 15 minutes as I dissected and dismissed each one of his objections. Finally, in an exasperated tone, he declared "you have peeled me like an onion and I am embarrassed to learn that I am prejudiced." He never attended another meeting but he never supported or opposed us.

One Friday afternoon I was visiting the property with Joel Weisenfeld, a WORC member, when a couple walked up to us. I will call them Mr. and Mrs. Legree.

"Mr. Schneps? We represent the Little Neck Community Association," he said.

"Really?" I smiled. "How long have you been with the Association?"

"Just a month. Why?"

"No reason."

Mr. Legree handed me a typed sheet of paper.

"We have prepared a list of 24 homes and properties we think would be just ideal for your purpose. We wish you would consider them as alternatives to this one."

Mrs. Legree added, "appropriate and available equivalent alternatives," and I could see those exact words typed atop the list. Joel and I exchanged a glance.

"Joel, have you got a map in the car?" I asked.

"I do."

"Well, let's take a look."

The Legrees shook our hands and rushed to their car.

I had lived in Queens for a while. I looked at the list, looked at the map, and said, "turn left at the corner."

The first property we saw could not accommodate more than two bedrooms, at most. The next two had no front, side, or rear yards. The next one was tiny, and also dilapidated. The State demanded at least eight people per home, refusing to accept my limitation of three beds.

The next was a vacant, undeveloped property that could not accommodate a group home even if we had the facilities to build one, which we did not.

And so on, too small, no yard, falling apart.

And my personal favorite, a narrow slither of mud, 300 feet long and 10 feet wide, along a parkway. It was neither available nor suitable for construction of any kind, unless you liked bowling.

So far, none of the addresses on the list was remotely appropriate, none an equivalent alternative to the house on Gaskel Road.

And then there was one.

A nice street, sun, trees and a yard on every side. It was big enough to have several bedrooms. We knocked at the door.

A man came to the screen door in baggy pants and an undershirt, holding the Daily News. "Yeah?"

"Is this house for sale?"

"No! Why?"

"I'm sorry." I looked at Joel. "Was it ever for sale?"

"Yeah. And I bought it…twelve years ago!" He slammed the door.

The opponents must have thought that it would take days or weeks to visit and evaluate so many properties. But the properties were so inappropriate as to make evaluation easy within 48 hours. I formally informed them that none of the properties were acceptable and I was no longer willing to participate in a fishing expedition.

We scheduled an open meeting for the community in an assembly hall. I would speak and answer any questions. Unfortunately, I had torn the plantaris muscle in my leg playing tennis the previous day. So, I made my entrance on crutches. Many of the attendees did not know me, and when I appeared I could hear them gasp.

"To those who do not know me," I said, "I hurt myself playing tennis. My apparent handicap is a temporary condition."

I could hear them let out their breath. The relief was palpable but my leg hurt like mad. Some laughed, a sort of, "Ha ha, who's afraid of the big bad wolf!"

The meeting ran four hours. I spoke. I answered questions. I cannot imagine I changed any minds. If I spoke well, supporters would be pleased. Opponents would see me as a cheap sideshow barker, a skilled con artist.

Finally, the opposition sought the help of Queens Borough President, Donald Manes. Mr. Manes scheduled an open meeting in his conference room in Queens Borough Hall, to discuss the matter. I had never met Mr. Manes. As far as I knew, he held the meeting under pressure from the opposition.

The conference room was packed against our small contingent. Some of the opponents were agitated and seemed to be aware that they were facing their final political opportunity. Mr. Manes was not yet present when the meeting was called to order.

"I'm concerned for the poor children," one woman said. "They'd have to navigate through traffic, snowstorms, ice storms…"

"And they'd have trouble with the community. Community opposition."

"And the neighborhood children. Children can be so cruel."

"We're not *against* the idea of community homes, just…"

One participant openly predicted that some retarded children could be injured if they live in the proposed group home. He was tall and broad. He stood up and faced me when he spoke.

"If you open that home it'll be dangerous for the mentally retarded."

I popped out of my seat and faced him. "Are you threatening the children who will be living in the group home? Are you threatening to injure any of those children? Tell me. Stand up here and tell me whether you are going to hurt any of those children."

The room went quiet. All eyes turned to him.

He did not speak again.

Mr. Manes swept into the meeting room and said "hello" to everyone. "Nice to see you, Murray," he added, though we had never met or spoken before. Then he asked me, "Are you willing to move the group home from the planned site to another location."

"No," I said. "We intend to utilize our existing site."

He faced all the attendees and said, "I asked him and he said 'no.' " Then he stood and left as suddenly and quickly as he had arrived. Was I shocked? Yes. Were they shocked? Absolutely. Everyone began to leave, quietly.

Quietness did not last long. Within an hour following the end of the meeting I got a telephone message from my secretary.

"Your daughter is in the hospital."

"Which daughter, where?"

"He didn't say."

"Who called? What hospital?"

"He just said that and hung up."

My heart rate doubled. First, I called Elizabeth's school and was reassured she was fine. Then, I inquired about Lara and found that she was fine as well.

The call was a hoax. I tried to catch my breath. Who was the target? Lara? Elizabeth? Me? In that horrible moment, I had to make a terrible decision - whom to call first - and I called Elizabeth. I am so sorry, Lara, that I did not choose you. I have spent decades trying to untie this knot. I still feel guilty. I would never have believed that I could choose one of my children over another. But only when one is presented with real choices, will remarkable truths be revealed.

It is telling that someone disrupted my life this much, for this many years, with so little effort.

It goes without saying that, once I entered into the Willowbrook struggles and the public battles, I knew I was going to make some enemies. At first I thought that they would have the courage to insult me to my face and to stay away from my family. Live and learn, as my mom loved to say.

I even got a special license plate with the name "SCHNEPS" across it so that no one could make a mistake and blow up the wrong car. If they wanted me, they could have me. The kids rode with Vicki.

It has been my experience in life that every person believes that he is ethical. The man who threatens violence to retarded children if the group home opens on his block, the man who leaves a bogus message that someone's child is in the hospital, both believe they are behaving ethically. Your ethics are not truly tested until you personally face some jeopardy or loss of some kind.

The Little Neck Community Association filed suit in the Supreme Court of the State of New York, County of Queens, against WORC, seeking to enjoin the agency from using a one-family residence as a group home for mentally retarded children. About that time, WORC closed title on the property. The board of directors was not willing to lose the site. Another available and appropriate location might not be easily found. As the agency was paying fair value for the property, the worst we could do was to resell the home without substantial loss.

Justice Angelo Graci was assigned the case and granted summary judgment in our favor, dismissing the complaint. He found that there were no triable issues of fact, that is, there was no case against us.

Justice Graci was the father of a mentally retarded child, so the attorneys for the plaintiff sought his recusal. Justice Graci refused to recuse himself. The opposition filed charges against him, alleging that Justice Graci had a conflict of interest. All charges against him were dismissed. The plaintiff appealed Justice Graci's order and the Appellate Division confirmed Justice Graci's order in a written opinion. In addition to determining and confirming that a group home for mentally retarded children is a permitted use in a single-family residential zone, the Court recognized that the plaintiffs were prejudiced by stating:

"(w)hile professing to be sympathetic to the plight of these unfortunate children, the appellants nevertheless suggest that the proposed group home should be located in a residential zone other than one restricted to single-family homes."

Not next to me. Not on my block. Not in my neighborhood.

I must acknowledge that the opponents unwittingly assisted us in reducing the number of beds in the group home from the original 15—the number insisted by the State—to eight. Our opponents yelled loudly enough, about the proposed number of residents and staff, to reach the ears of some politicians like Sen. Padavan and the State reduced the size. I was thrilled. Previously the State had offered us a "15 beds or none" deal. We hated the offer but were committed to opening the group home. I am pleased to note that the group home continues to operate an excellent program, offering a real life to its residents. Although not all neighbors approve of the group home, many have accepted its existence and are good neighbors to the mentally retarded residents. Not a single negative incident has occurred.

20

A CONFERENCE

On Friday, January 23, 1976, I appeared at a conference held by the Rose F. Kennedy Center and the Bronx Mental Retardation Council, at the Albert Einstein College of Medicine, to make a presentation regarding Willowbrook. Too much misinformation was being disseminated and I welcomed the opportunity to educate a few hundred people who were in the field. In order to do that I had to give my audience a history lesson first, then talk about the present system and, finally, our plans for the future. I hoped they would see that we did not want to take away any services or jobs from one group to give to another. We wanted everyone under the same tent.

I reminded everyone that, at the time of the class action, "we were facing a budget crisis that had resulted in a cruel and inhumane job freeze. This job freeze has decimated the already demoralized direct care staff at all of the New York State institutions for the mentally retarded, including Willowbrook." A quick reduction of direct care staff occurred because, as the overworked attendants resigned, no one could be hired to replace them. This resulted in unprecedented numbers of deaths at accelerated rates. Even Dr. Hammond, the former Director of Willowbrook, had complained that children at Willowbrook were dying as a result of under staffing and he was without the ability to stop the process.

I also informed the attendees that the Willowbrook case was designed and instituted to dismantle the institutional system and to replace it with a community-based system. This new system would develop individualized services to meet the needs of individual human beings, in the "least restrictive environment possible." I explained the meaning of a consent judgment, the function of the Willowbrook Review Panel and emphasized that the panel interpreted the term "possible" to mean "required and appropriate for the resident," while the Department of Mental Hygiene insisted that the term "possible" meant "available." Of course, if "possible" meant "available," we would have had an empty victory.

I tried to make them see that it would be a struggle to implement the Willowbrook Consent Judgment. As the fisherman in Hemingway's *The Old Man and the Sea* knew well, hooking the fish was not enough. The road home can be a long and treacherous journey, with no guarantee of a fulfilling meal.

I reminded this group of professionals that the problem of implementation was complicated by the existing dual system for the care, treatment, and habilitation of the mentally retarded: the institution system was owned and operated by the State and the community programs were essentially operated by voluntary agencies. The State and Federal governments funded both systems and they were presumably obligated to provide oversight to both. The dual system permitted both systems to operate side-by-side, without treading on each other's hallowed ground.

My goal was for them to see for themselves that the existing dual system divided those needing services into two different groups of mentally retarded people: "ours" (those in the institutions) and "theirs" (those in the community). The existence of "ours" and "theirs" resulted in a competition for the same pot of public funds. Obviously, the "ours" had the organization, the money, and the political influence to fight for a bigger share. The "theirs" did not.

During the budget crisis in the 1970s many advocates managing the voluntary agencies struggled for more funding. Rather than pressing to change our system to a unified single system, the voluntary agencies mortally feared that the Willowbrook Consent Judgment, and especially the Willowbrook Review Panel, would move more money to the institutions rather than to their community programs.

Perhaps that is why a few leaders got it in their minds that we wanted to move more funds to institutions and away from their programs, and led to certain community agency leaders, like Jerry Weingold of the New York State Association for Retarded Children and Helen Kaplan of the Nassau County Association for Retarded Children, to oppose the Willowbrook Review Panel.

I made it clear that nothing was further from the truth. In fact, that would have been the exact opposite of our goals.

Unfortunately, too many attendees viewed my words as impractical projections of a mere fantasy. They were comfortable with the existing bureaucracy. A few approached me and shared their view and hope of a new order of things that could and should be achieved. In spite of the fact that I was unable to convert the devotees of the institutional paradigm, I was merely amazed and surprised but not depressed or dissuaded from my beliefs. Instead, my efforts were accelerated.

When the conference ended, I drove from the Bronx to the Richmond Children Center to pick up Lara and bring her home for the weekend. As always, seeing and being with Lara was a priority in our lives. Our visits kept the struggles and the long hours in perspective. My Lara was safe and all these children should be safe as well.

21

SAMANTHA

And life does not slow down just because you are busy.

Whatever the 70s meant to the rest of the world, to us it meant trying to have a third baby. We had been trying almost since Elizabeth's birth in 1970, and now it was 1976. Lovemaking became less fun and more like an Olympic competition. We had a life at home with the kids, my life as a lawyer, my work with the Panel, Vicki's life as a graduate student and teacher. And then we had our Olympic schedule of checking ovulation thermometers, sperm counts, monthly periods and tears of sad frustration. Once, I inadvertently entered our bathroom at the moment when Vicki discovered that she was, again, *not* pregnant. I came as close as it was possible for a man to understand what that felt like. After all our efforts, and it seemed crazy to think of making love as an "effort," she broke into tears, as if her body was playing some sick joke on her.

Our plight took us to a well-known gynecologist, a purported "genius," who convinced us that Vicki had a tilted uterus and that surgery was required to correct the tilt.

I had heard of a face lift, but a uterus lift? The world was changing. What did I know? Following the surgery, while Vicki was recovering at home, one of the sutures broke and she almost died from a hemorrhage. A neighbor found her in the elevator and called the police. A New York City Police officer picked her up, rushed her to the Long Island Jewish Hospital and saved her life. The hospital called my office in lower Manhattan. I hailed a cab.

I said, "one hundred dollars if you get me to Long Island Jewish Hospital in 30 minutes."

Best $100 I ever spent.

Vicki was difficult to see in the bed. She was almost as white as the sheets. I leaned close to her.

She whispered, "I knew you'd be here."

I had been handling a medical malpractice case, and I needed a consult from an OB/GYN. That is how I met Eulogio Jerez, MD., or "E" (his name to friends). Through a stroke of luck or an act of G-d, Vicki became pregnant in early 1976. We determined that "E" would deliver the baby.

E agreed that I could witness the birth, a new idea then. I suited up in surgical garb. My mother would have been so proud!

Samantha was born on the early morning of November 27, 1976. The birth went off without a hitch and we brought home another beautiful girl, her hair soft , reddish-blonde and gleaming. Our announcement blasted the words, "GIRLS, GIRLS, GIRLS — Lara and Elizabeth introduce our most recent girl, Samantha Rachel."

Now, Lara would have another person to love her forever.

22

SUFFOLK DEVELOPMENTAL CENTER

I was on a quest to close large warehousing institutions and move the residents to group homes. The next opportunity presented itself.

The Suffolk Developmental Center ("Suffolk") was a State-owned and operated institution for the mentally retarded, located in Melville. Melville is located in the middle of Long Island, about an hour's drive from Manhattan. In 1978, a time when I was well known by many parents as being a fierce advocate for retarded children, parents of the children at Suffolk and its parent organization, the Society for Good Will to Retarded Children, Inc. ("Society"), began interviewing attorneys. They wanted someone to represent their children in a suit to secure benefits similar to those secured in the Willowbrook Consent Judgment. Suffolk was a relatively new facility and was opening a new baby building but its conditions were worse than Willowbrook. Its administrators and direct care staff seemed to lack knowledge and interest. The degree of idleness and lack of interaction made it the saddest institution I ever saw. When its new baby building was opening we had been offered the choice of transferring Lara from Willowbrook to Suffolk, which was much closer to our home. We visited the facility and easily rejected that "opportunity." No thanks.

At my interview for the job, I sat before the Society board of directors as they smiled and fired questions at me.

"When were you admitted to the bar?"

"Tell us about your work as a litigator."

"What cases have you handled relating to the mentally retarded?"

I must have answered to their satisfaction because they were still smiling when they said, "Thank you for coming."

That was when I said, "Now *I* have some questions."

They stopped smiling.

"What?"

"Exactly what kind of relief are you seeking for your children?"

A few exchanged glances. One woman began speaking, with no particular destination in mind, never a wise idea. "We, uh, want…." She trailed off.

"Mr. Schneps. Are you saying you might not take the case, even if we want to retain you?"

"That is exactly what I am saying." A few jaws dropped. I went on. "If you are seeking an improved institution, a better, cleaner Suffolk Developmental Center, I am not your guy. I will not represent you. If you are seeking and willing to fight for community placement for all mentally retarded individuals living at Suffolk, except for those who require hospitalization, I am your man. Otherwise, I am not interested."

There was a long silence, and a huddle. Finally, one of them spoke. "Yes, that's…that's exactly what we want."

"Which?" I asked.

"Placement."

I was retained.

It shocked me that some parents refused to become named plaintiffs or participate in the litigation, including one who was an attorney and represented the interests of mentally retarded individuals and their parents. Although he was fully prepared to garner all benefits that might flow, he would not lend his name to the suit. Obviously, not every parent had the same level of commitment. Not every person handles fear in the same manner. Some feared reprisals against their children. Fear seemed to be universal in such institutions. I had to be wary, as some parents liked to appear to be everyone's friend, whether they were friend or foe, supportive or not. Others feared the experience of testifying on the witness stand. Many people feared that cross-examination would make them appear foolish or worse.

I selected a number of named plaintiffs based upon both the histories of their children, as well as my judgment as to what kind of a witness each would be.

Using a detailed questionnaire, notes of interviews, letters and copies of records, I prepared the federal class action complaint. When the parents accepted my complaint, the action was filed before the United States District Court, Eastern District of New York. I immediately learned that the case was assigned to Judge Jack B. Weinstein. I felt a sudden lightness. Judge Weinstein was known to be a liberal, bright, progressive, creative, and sensitive judge. I did a little jig at the counter of the Court Clerk. Malachy would have been proud.

Back when the Willowbrook Class Action had been commenced, Bruce Ennis hoped that Judge Jack B. Weinstein would be assigned to that case. Following the death of Judge Orrin G. Judd, we again hoped that Judge Weinstein would get the assignment. Instead, Judge John R. Bartels got the case. In fact, we were very lucky to have had Judge Bartels. He was the perfect judge for the Willowbrook case.

The Suffolk action was filed in 1978, three years after the Willowbrook Consent Judgment. I had been Vice Chairman of the Willowbrook Review Panel for more than three years and was not a favorite of the State of New York or its Department of Mental Hygiene.

So, the State retained, at considerable cost, a major international law firm specializing in litigation, LeBoeuf, Lamb, Leiby & MacRae, Esqs. Their mission: to prepare and prosecute a proceeding before Judge Weinstein seeking to remove Murray B. Schneps, as either the attorney for the plaintiffs in the Suffolk case or, alternatively, as a member of the Willowbrook Review Panel.

Schneps in the crosshairs.

If they thought it was possible to remove me from both positions, they would have taken a shot. My removal as either attorney for the plaintiffs in the Suffolk

Developmental Center, or as a member of the Willowbrook Review Panel, might cause critical damage to whichever case I was removed from. This was not a matter of ego, it was a matter of fact. And I was not the only one who thought so.

"You're a gladiator," one ally said after watching me in court. "But you're *our* gladiator."

I took the motion to remove me seriously. Christopher Hansen, Esq., of the New York Civil Liberties Union, agreed to represent me, and to represent my clients during the period of time the removal was pending against me. Oral argument was scheduled before Judge Weinstein.

The oral argument was held on October 26, 1978, two months before my 41st birthday. Many friends, family, and clients packed the courtroom. There was also a large contingent of administration and staff members from both the Department of Mental Hygiene and the Suffolk Developmental Center. It was a carnival-type atmosphere, nervousness and excitement filled the air. My supporters greeted each other with cheerful anticipation and expectation of a victory for Murray and the good guys. Normally when people enter a courtroom, especially a Federal courtroom, they are immediately stricken with calm reserve. The buzz in the room persisted until Judge Weinstein entered the courtroom and sat in his high backed chair before the bench. Judge Weinstein, a tall, slim, handsome man with straight black hair streaked in silver, rapped his gavel and stated: "Order please. I will hear argument on the Society motion at the end of the calendar."

When our case was called, the State's "hired gun" made an unpleasant characterization about me. "Murray B. Schneps, this Janus-faced attorney, must be disqualified in this case or removed from the Willowbrook Review Panel, as he creates an appearance of impropriety, unfairness to the defendants, and is unethical."

There was a shout from the crowd, a single voice. "How dare ye speak that way. Shove it up yer arse, ye lying corporate bastard!"

Gales of laughter came from the crowd. Judge Weinstein pounded his gavel.

"If there are any further outcries, I'll clear the court."

There were none. And though I will not say who was responsible for that particular outcry, I will say it was cried out in an Irish accent and that Malachy McCourt was present at the time.

Chris Hansen presented excellent oral argument before the Court. "The removal of this experienced competent counsel will negatively affect the rights and interests of handicapped people. Such removal will render it more and more difficult, if not impossible, to vindicate the rights of such mentally retarded individuals. The retarded need and require counsel like Mr. Schneps to protect their interests."

When all argument was finished, Judge Weinstein rose. "Will the attorneys join me in Chambers."

In his Chambers, the judge turned to me. "You'll be required to choose whether to withdraw as attorney in the Suffolk Developmental Center case or as a member of the Willowbrook Review Panel."

There was a long silence. Finally, I said, "Do you want a response from me?"

"Yes! Yes, I want a response from you."

I said, "I have made my decision but I will not reveal my thoughts in the presence of my adversaries. I will await the Court's decision."

When we left the conference it seemed a foregone conclusion that Judge Weinstein would require me to withdraw as attorney for the plaintiffs in the Suffolk Developmental Center case or as a member of the Willowbrook Review Panel. An appeal would follow. On January 9, 1979, before Judge Weinstein ruled, the United States Circuit Court, Second Circuit, rendered a decision in the *Board of Education of the City of New York v. Nyquist,* a case with which I was not involved. The Court stated that "(U)nless an attorney's conduct tends to 'taint the underlying trial; . . . by disturbing the balance of the presentations" the court should be "quite hesitant to disqualify an attorney." I was buoyed by the Federal Appellate Court decision and felt that Judge Weinstein would have great difficulty in removing me as either attorney for the plaintiffs in the Society case or member of the Willowbrook Review Panel. No judge wants to be reversed.

On February 21, 1979, Judge Jack B. Weinstein issued his decision. He denied the defendants' motion to disqualify me and remove me as either the attorney for the plaintiffs in the Suffolk case or as a member of the Willowbrook Review Panel. Timing was everything and Judge Weinstein could not disregard the ruling made by the

Federal Court of Appeals. He was careful to note that protecting individual rights sometimes required flexibility in formulating changes to complex societal institutions. He then went on to determine that the defendants' position, that I was somehow incapable of doing both jobs fairly, was without merit.

More important to me was his clear statement that my considerable expertise and commitment in representing the rights of the mentally retarded children was unparalleled in the legal community and that my position on the Review Panel was never intended to be one of neutrality. Of course I was partisan on behalf of my clients, he expected no less, and such strident advocacy did not create any conflict of interest. Further, my expertise as to the substance and implementation of children's rights, gained as a member of the Review Panel, was a basis for my qualification for the Suffolk case, not disqualification.

Judge Weinstein then brushed aside the defendants' concerns that the State would face a "whipsaw" problem with me as an attorney-adversary in the Suffolk case and as a Willowbrook Review Panel member. He recognized that I had always been their adversary and soothed the defendants' potential fears by sarcastically assuring them that "(t)his court is confident that Mr. Schneps will not be able to coerce the sovereign State of New York or its counsel. Should they feel incapable of resisting such pressure as he may generate, they may appeal to the court for protection."

His words felt like a belated birthday gift.

I was happy and satisfied to continue as a member of the Willowbrook Review Panel and to act as attorney for the plaintiffs in the Suffolk case.

Preparing the Suffolk trial included three years of discovery proceedings, which is essentially an exchange of available information between the two sides. I had to secure information and records from the State and had to conduct oral depositions of State employees and administrators. In turn, the State's attorneys deposed some of our witnesses. The State never responded promptly to requests and dragged out deposition and discovery dates in accordance with its game plan of delay.

Several weeks prior to the commencement of the actual trial, I asked my friend and cohort at the Willowbrook Review Panel, Mike Lottman, to partner with me. Until that point, I had essentially acted alone. One attorney against two large major law offices—the office of the Attorney General of the State of New York and the law offices of LeBoeuf, Lamb, Leiby & MacRae—too much for one lawyer. I was asking for trouble. I had to admit it. Even with two of us, it was a daunting task. But the cause was worthy and Mike agreed to join me. We had a lot of knowledge and experience and worked well together. As a team, we had an indefatigable energy. The impossible seemed possible.

In the last week before the trial commenced, Mike and I worked as much as 15 to 20 hours each day. We identified our witnesses, including the parents, residents, employees, defendants, and experts. We divided the list of witnesses and identified and copied all required documents, thousands of pages. We also organized hundreds of photographs I had taken at Suffolk Developmental Center during the visits conducted with our experts.

On the first day of the trial, I offered as the first witness, James Clements, M.D. Jim was the Chairman of the Willowbrook Review Panel and was an eminent expert in the field. We utilized Jim's testimony to provide two-fold critical evidence. He was to introduce the institution and then to educate the Court regarding mental retardation, the residents, and their needs and the conditions.

But Judge Weinstein seemed to be in a rush to get the case finished as quickly as possible. Even before the trial began, it was my sense that Judge Weinstein had already determined what relief he was planning to grant. Interesting point: from the beginning, the State's attorneys insisted that I was seeking the closure of the institution. "Nonsense," I argued. "I never asked for that! The complaint never mentions closing the institution." Yet they insisted that is what I wanted, and the judge believed it. My ploy fooled no one. I was a well-known entity.

Of course it was true. Anyone who ever met me, shook my hand, tested my blood, or heard me in any one of dozens of TV interviews, knew that I saw institutions as hopeless. Of course I wanted the place closed. But I never asked for it. I simply sought appropriate conditions for all class members in the institution, including community placement when it was appropriate. Perhaps it was easy for anyone to notice that Jim Clements found that *no one* actually required institutionalization. The relief I sought would result in emptying the institution. Once everyone who was appropriate for community placement was placed, few people, if any, would be left in the institution. Under such circumstances, it would not be necessary for the Court to order the closing of the institution, as the State would do so. Maintaining an all but empty institution could not be economically justified.

During his testimony, Jim Clements testified to the Court that he compared Suffolk with other institutions he had inspected and repeated his observations and opinions that the Suffolk Developmental Center was "a place of idleness." He said, and other experts agreed, that it was a worse place than Willowbrook despite the fact that its buildings were relatively new. The Suffolk Developmental Center was a scary place. There seemed to be a total lack of interaction between the residents and staff, and between staff members. The direct care staff did not get off their chairs, even when experts and counsel arrived to inspect the entire facility. This was true even though all staff members were repeatedly given notice of all inspections. It was obvious they had no training and had no idea what their function should have been.

At the trial, immediately following Jim Clements' testimony, Mike and I made a request that Judge Weinstein, along with the attorneys and experts, visit and evaluate the institution in person at any time or day, without prior notice to anyone. The State attorneys objected and demanded seven days advance notice for any visits. Finally, Judge Weinstein permitted us to visit with two days notice.

There would be no surprise visits but two days suited us just fine, as they could never convert a pig's ear to a silk purse in two days. Since the State selected the buildings to visit, we also worried that, maybe, we were being set up.

When we arrived, the place looked like the institution in "One Flew Over the Cuckoo's Nest," with clean, smooth white sheets, clean floors and an overabundance of nurses wearing starched white uniforms and tidy caps. The place looked efficient and almost pleasant.

But the truth prevailed and, after an hour or so, the façade began to collapse. When Judge Weinstein agreed to visit a building we suggested, he agreed and we entered the authentic institution. The false curtain dissolved and the real Suffolk Developmental Center became crystal clear. The usual smells were no longer disguised by air sanitizers and the idleness, broken chairs, sparse furniture, and the clients sitting and lying on terrazzo floors, unattended and unsupervised, could not be hidden. I secretly smiled inside and Judge Weinstein's face sank. From that moment on, Judge Weinstein seemed to be evaluating what relief he would grant rather than who would win the case.

We thought that Jim Clements' testimony would take the entire first day. When Judge Weinstein stepped on the gas and Jim finished quickly, we called our back-up witness but that exhausted our plan for the next day. At the end of the first trial day, we did not have any other witnesses prepared, lined up, or ready to testify for the next morning.

The judge knew where he was going and was in a hurry to get there. There was no stopping him. From the courthouse in Brooklyn, I called all the parent witnesses and told them to meet us at the home of Russell Cohen's parents in Suffolk County. Lila Cohen was the president of the parent organization. "It's an emergency," I said.

At the meeting, we explained the situation. "We'll have to begin parent testimony tomorrow."

"No."

"I can't."

"Absolutely not."

One mother sitting near me turned white. It was clear there were a variety of reasons for not wanting to appear on the stand a day ahead of schedule, but fear was chief among them.

Mike almost fainted. I said, "Listen. You have to testify tomorrow morning. This is your time to stand up and be counted. This is it. *There will be no other date or time.* We have worked on this for years. Without your testimony, we will be in default and the case will be dismissed. Explain that to your kids."

There was a long, uncomfortable silence.

"O.K., I'll do it."

"I'll…I'll be there."

"I guess."

I turned to the woman who had gone pale at the prospect of appearing on the witness stand. Much as I lived my life at the center of things, I knew there were people who would rather do anything than be looked at, much less prodded with questions. I was pretty sure she was one of them but suddenly she burst into tears, then nodded. I knew she was in.

It was unanimous. They would all appear.

Mike and I divided up the witnesses and prepared each parent for testimony.

The next morning each witness gave excellent testimony and faced limited, if any, cross-examination.

One of my favorite witnesses, a father who had an adult daughter residing at Suffolk, gave the following testimony:

Q. What seemed to happen to Susan after she entered the institution?

A. She seemed to regress. She seemed to sit more and sleep more and go into herself instead of being outgoing. Like she normally was.

Q. Was she ever toilet trained during her time at Suffolk Developmental Center?

A. She was toilet trained *before* she went in. She started to wet and she started to soil herself.

Q. And did that continue during her year at Suffolk Developmental Center?

A. Yes, it did.

Q. Susan recently moved into and now lives in a small group home?

A. Yes, she does.

Q. How is she doing in the group home?

A. She is doing really well and the change that has come over Susan, it's like night and day. In six weeks there was a big change.

She does things that I never thought was humanly possible. I didn't think that Susan could make the bed. They have helped her a lot and now she is proud to make her own bed.

She is learning how to dress herself. She has her own drawer, brand new drawers, new plates, a new bed. And she places her clothes and everything away.

She takes her own showers. She washes her own hair. I never thought Susan would have a key to be able to open a door. She can open the door herself. She goes out and they take her shopping.

She is living like a human being.

I just can't express how beautiful it is. It is a tremendous weight off both my wife and my shoulders.

I have always worried about what Susan would do, how she would live, when I am not here. I am going on 68 and who knows when I may meet my maker.

And it is just the most beautiful thing that ever happened. Susan is a human being. She is living like a human being. She is happy.

After he took several photographs of Susan out of his wallet and displayed them to Judge Weinstein, he said, "Thank you, Your Honor" and burst with joy saying:

> I don't know how I can explain it. She has come up so much. She talks like a blue streak. She understands things.
>
> I never thought Susan - - I must admit I sold Susan short. I, as a parent, sold Susan short. I didn't know she had the ability, although I knew she had the ability to go further than she was. But I never thought where she could go where she is now.
>
> My daughter is now a woman.

The State called Judy Walker to appear and testify. Judy was the Nursing Program Coordinator at Suffolk Developmental Center and a very tough adversary. However, Judy and I became well acquainted during the numerous inspections held at Suffolk Developmental Center with plaintiffs' experts. She was designated by the State to shadow me and see what I was doing. In time, we developed a mutual respect and friendship as she learned to appreciate our position and to view the conditions at the institution from our point of view. She accepted the appropriateness of our goal to place all residents from the institutions into small residential homes. During her direct testimony on behalf of the State (her employee) it became clear to me that Judy was following the State's line that all was well with the institution and its residents and it was not necessary for the Court to be involved in the operation and management of the institution. The responsibility to cross-examine Judy Walker fell to me. During cross-examination my approach was to begin a conversation between us, as colleagues, in order to dismantle the wall constructed between us. In time, she became less and less defensive and truthfully answered soft questions. Since she had attended every inspection with me and my experts, walking side by side with me and viewing each and every photograph as I took it, she was easily able to acknowledge that each photograph offered into evidence was a true and accurate representations of what was depicted. We spoke of the needs of the residents in the institution and she readily agreed that community placement was suitable and beneficial to most of the residents. When I realized that Judy was again amenable to speak more freely and truthfully, without being defensive, I asked her if she agreed that even if adequately trained staff, health and medical professionals and habilitation and other specialists were provided "the real place they should be is in the community and … not in the institution … a place for them to blossom?" She simply answered, "from your mouth to G-d's ear." Further questions were no longer necessary and I ended my cross-examination.

In spite of the fact that Judge Weinstein did not grant plaintiffs all of the benefits we sought, including an extensive order directing community placement, the Suffolk Developmental Center was ultimately closed. Even without gaining a proper community placement order, the closing of the institution was a major victory.

Vicki and I rejoiced and so did my children to the degree they were able to appreciate it. I am sure Lara would have enjoyed my dance and song of victory if she could but, mostly, she was just happy to be in her daddy's arms.

23

JOSHUA

While the motion to disqualify me was being waged we learned that another blessing was going to be added to the family. Vicki and I were thrilled to know we would be welcoming another child.

Sweet Lara was then living at the Richmond Center in Mount Vernon, just 30 minutes from our home. While the Richmond Children Center was not our ideal home for Lara, it was getting closer to the place we envisioned. It had approximate 50 young profoundly retarded multiply handicapped children housed in an extremely large home with bedrooms holding 4 to 6 children in each bedroom. More importantly, they provided trained direct care staff, plus some therapy. We still yearned for a truly small facility – three or fewer beds – close to our home, with a real therapeutic program. My ultimate fantasy was Lara's return to our home.

In the ten years since Lara's birth in 1968, science had progressed a great deal. Amniocentesis had become a standard procedure. Our OB/GYN, Dr. Eulogio Jerez, "E", agreed that he would deliver our next child as soon as the amniotic fluid established that the baby's lungs were mature. We were grateful for this new tool and E performed an amniocentesis about a month before the baby was due.

There was one proviso, we told E that we did not want to know the sex of the baby until the time of birth. Science would not rob us of the ability to shout the news "It's a boy!" or "It's a girl!" That said, E knew we were hoping for a boy. Carrying on the Schneps name was something I hoped to do for my father. I had chosen the name Joshua, if I had a son, after a sweet and engaging toddler I knew when I was ten years old. That is when I had settled on the name.

For all E's gifts as a physician, he was lousy at keeping a secret.

E called us on a Sunday night. Vicki picked up the phone, and E told her the baby was a boy. Vicki began to cry.

Elizabeth was eight. "Mommy, what's wrong?"

"Nothing's wrong Lizzie."

"Why are you crying?"

"It's just…that…the baby's a boy!"

With some persuasion, Elizabeth agreed to keep the secret. Our secret was safe, until she got angry with us.

"I'm telling! I'm telling everybody! The baby is a boy. Named Joshua."

I said, "Go ahead. You will not hurt us. It will only hurt you."

"Why?"

"Because if you tell our secret, you won't hurt me or Mommy. You'll only hurt yourself."

"How will I hurt myself?"

"Because, if you tell this secret, it will be very hard for me to ever tell you a secret again."

She considered this seriously. And she did not tell anyone.

My eight year-old daughter could keep a secret but Dr. Eulogio Jerez could not.

On November 2, 1978, we visited Dr. Jerez at the hospital for the performance of an amniocentesis. I had attended each visit and observed each amniocentesis. As he withdrew the fluid, I noted that the amniotic fluid was a light greenish color rather than being colorless. I knew that this was a sign that my son may be or had been in distress. E sat straight up, immediately phoned for an operating room, called an anesthesiologist, and told Vicki and I that he was going to deliver Joshua immediately. The nurses wheeled Vicki to the operating room. E ran to the physicians' lockers. "Follow me," he said. I ran after him and I also changed into the surgeon greens.

He assured me, "your son is fine."

My fear was not assuaged. I said, "if you want me to leave the operating room for any reason, I will leave." We marched into the operating room.

When E lifted Joshua out of the uterus, I noticed that his little fingernails were stained green. My heart sunk and I immediately thought of Lara. Had we not been punished enough?

In spite of E's further assurances, the presence of meconium in the amniotic fluid and the amniotic stained nails, left me in a controlled panic. I watched Joshua like a hawk. He seemed to be doing very well. He was alert, sucked and breathed very well. Soon he was focusing on our eyeballs. Fortunately, Joshua sustained no problems. While in the hospital I overheard Vicki tell someone about the meconium stains and state that, "Murray always knows."

In our announcement to the world that Joshua was born, we mailed the words: "WE DID IT. OUR BUTTONS ARE BURSTING!"

And, of course: "IT'S A BOY!"

Approximately one year later, E asked me how my son was doing and confessed that he had been scared to death, especially when he saw the meconium stained fingernails. But I was delighted to report that Joshua was doing great.

24

BUILDING ON THE FACTS

It is my belief that if institutions were eliminated and replaced with group homes, the issues of overcrowding, understaffing, and exploding budgets would disappear. Maintaining large institutions requires an overall staff ratio of one resident to one staff member, in order to provide coverage 24 hours a day, 365 days a year. In a group home or other small community residential facility, the overall ratio is less than one-to-one, while providing better coverage. All staff in the group home are hands-on providers of direct care services to the residents. For example, at Willowbrook with 5,700 residents, a one-to-one ratio, including a large contingent of administrators who provided no hands-on services, would require a staff of 5,700. To the uneducated, or uncaring, such large staff numbers made it easy for the State budget cutters to reduce the minimum staff of 5,700 by 500 to 1000, resulting in a total staff of 5,200 to 4,700, and at the same time leave a "sense" that there remained sufficient staff to operate properly.

But such thinking resulted in a dangerous illusion. Insufficient staff immediately results in the deterioration of all aspects of every residential facility. In a small community residential home or apartment with three to eight residents, with three to eight staff, it is obvious that cutting the staff by even ten percent would be devastating. It would not occur. Small residential homes are easier to manage, easier to observe and evaluate, and easier to analyze and correct. Moreover, non-partisan analysis showed that the annual cost per resident in small community residence is less than *one half* of the annual cost per resident in an institution. Better care at a reduced cost make the idea of cutting of the budget unnecessary and unreasonable.

In handling any litigation an attorney must first learn all of the facts and the law applicable to a specific case. Where the case has important aspects requiring special knowledge and expertise, the attorney must also educate the judge and the jury. This is particularly true in cases involving the handicapped.

The need to educate was strikingly apparent during the Suffolk Developmental Center trial. Our goal was to give the judge a real sense of the needs of mentally retarded people. We had a story to tell and I knew that whoever tells the best story wins. We presented experts who operated both large institutions and small community residences to demonstrate the remarkable improvements made by mentally retarded people when they are placed from an institution to a group home. They showed that mentally retarded children were just like all of our children and needed the same things. They should not be punished for limitations foisted upon them by fate and were entitled to be cared for, protected and loved, and exercised and educated to the best of their abilities, just like all children.

I asked one parent, Margaret, about the condition she found her son, Peter, in when she visited him at Suffolk. Margaret spoke of Peter's isolation and sadness, his physical neglect and his lack of fresh air and sunshine. His lethargy was so apparent that she thought he was ill. But Peter was fortunate; he was placed in a group home. Margaret saw a different child then. Peter was happy to see her, happy to be outside, and happy to engage in exercises that sought to give him independent mobility. Progress was gradual but it was progress.

Stories of parents who were promised care and therapy at Suffolk Developmental Center and then saw their child's conditions deteriorate were hard to ignore. We hoped it would awaken the parent in anyone, especially the judge who was being asked to change those conditions.

Jim Clemens had testified that idleness and boredom in large institutions creates horrific behaviors, including self-stimulation. Self-stimulation can lead to self-inflicted mutilation. Self-inflicted pain can replace feeling nothing at all.

But nothing could have told that like the story of one teenager named Bobby. His father, Herb, testified that one afternoon he went to visit Bobby a few months after he went to live at Suffolk. Over those few months Bobby had become less engaged and more withdrawn.

"I entered the ward and heard a hollow, sharp sound, almost like a loud clock. I never heard a sound like that and when I followed it I discovered that Bobby was making that noise. He was punching himself in the face! I felt sick at the sound and sight of my son abusing himself. And I felt shocked that no one was trying to help him. I ran to him and held him in my arms and began to cry. I will never be the same after seeing my son hurting himself."

A few very brave and committed staff members also supported the reality that we painted. The hundreds of black and white photographs I had taken demonstrated the lack of care, the lack of human engagement, the lack of color and the lack of clean air and sunshine. Dickens had nothing on the reality that was the Suffolk Developmental Center.

Even more poignant was the truth that even profoundly retarded multi-handicapped children had a better quality of life and do better when placed in small group homes. Whatever progress they were capable of, large or small, whatever smile, or laugh, or joy they could show was enhanced when they got the proper care and nurturing. Is not that what we want for every human being?

I felt confident that my education process had been successful when I was about to cross-examine the State's first witness. I knew I was ready and, more importantly, Judge Weinstein was ready.

The State's attorney arose and announced his next witness. "I call Edward Jennings to the stand."

The door opened, people shuffled in their seats and Ed Jennings entered the courtroom. Ed was about six feet tall, blond hair, fair skin and slim. He was a high-level administrator, a former Director at Willowbrook and an expert in mental retardation still employed by the New York State Office of Mental Retardation and Developmental Disabilities.

I was ready for my cross-examination. Even though he had worked at Willowbrook, I knew, liked, and respected Ed. But he worked for *them*. I had previously taken his oral deposition in this case and secured several damaging admissions from him. He was under considerable pressure from the State and its attorneys not to waver from their script. As Ed walked to the witness stand, he passed my chair. I said, "Good morning, Ed."

He whispered, "I'm sorry, Murray."

He answered every question posed by the State's attorney crisply and without hesitation. He had been carefully prepared by the State and provided the answers it sought. I was fearful that he would be forced to offer testimony solely supportive to his employers. But I knew he was an honorable man and I played to his knowledge of institutions rather than trying to challenge his credibility.

I presented various questions relating to the conditions at Suffolk that could not be disputed; overcrowding, insufficient staff, inadequate physical and occupational therapists. Many have said that a lawyer should never ask a question when he does not know what the answer will be. I do not ascribe to that rule. Some answers benefit you either way and makes the witness look ridiculous. I dealt with the understaffing, overcrowding and lack of services. Only a fool would deny the undeniable.

Q. Does Suffolk Developmental Center house more residents than its designated census?

A. Yes. But we are working at reducing the population.

Q. Then Suffolk is overcrowded at this time?

A. It will not be.

Q. But, it is currently overcrowded, isn't it?

A. Yes it is.

Q. Does Suffolk Developmental Center employ the required number of direct care staff?

A. We continue to hire more people.

Q. But, you do not have a full complement of staff?

A. No.

Q. Did you ever?

A. No.

Q. You concede, do you not, that Suffolk Developmental Center is understaffed?

A. Yes.

Q. In direct care staff?

A. Yes.

Q. You would agree, would you not that it is critical for the protection of the residents to have a full complement of direct care staff?

A. I agree.

Q. Suffolk Developmental Center maintains a chart for the minimal number of direct care staff to be in attendance on each shift, in each ward, in each residential building?

A. Yes it does.

Q. And these charts identify the minimal number as being the critical number for each ward on each shift in all residential buildings?

A. Yes they do.

Q. Can you identify these documents that were previously admitted into evidence and verify that these are the records from Suffolk Developmental Center reflecting its minimal numbers for direct care staff for each ward, on each shift, in each building and reports of the actual attendance records for each ward, shift and building?

A. Yes. I can identify them all.

Q. And these records are true and accurate?

A. Yes.

Q. These records establish that many wards on many shifts operated at lower than the critical or minimal numbers for the direct care staff?

A. Yes they did.

When Ed Jennings time and again answered "yes" to the truth and accuracy of the photographs presented, the records proving endless injuries and many deaths, the number of residents compared with the number of staff, the lack of medical and dental examinations, and lack of teachers and therapists, and the smell and the idleness, it was easy to anticipate that an educated Judge Weinstein would intercede and ask questions directly to Ed Jenkins. And he did.

Judge Weinstein asked the pivotal question:

> Q. Given adequate functioning of personal management, physical facilities and the like, can you set up an institution of 900 people in Suffolk on these premises, that can do a decent job for people in the institution?

I had been fearful of asking that question of Ed but Judge Weinstein was able to raise the key and basic issue in the case: is it possible to operate a decent institution? As he was the Judge, a man of great authority, who could imprison someone for not telling the truth on trial, it was much more likely that a truthful and honest answer would follow. It would have been much easier for Ed Jennings to evade my questions but accurate and truthful answers were more readily provided to the Court. Mr. Jennings made the following response to the Court:

> A. I don't believe there is any historical record at all that that kind of resource, a facility of that kind, can be managed properly. You know, again, I don't believe we have a record of where a facility of that kind, given all that it needs, can be operated successfully.

Without having an educated Judge, such testimony would not have been elicited from that witness.

It was a sweet moment. The good guys won.

25

MAINTAINING THE STATUS QUO

The chief function of the Willowbrook Review Panel was to monitor and ensure the implementation of all of the provisions of the Willowbrook Consent Judgment and develop a community placement plan. We filed reports to the Court at least every six months, evaluating the progress and making suggestions. At that point, regular surveys were being conducted and reported by our staff both for Willowbrook and the related institutions, where other class members had been transferred, as well as the community residences operating throughout the five boroughs of the City of New York, as well as Nassau, Suffolk and Westchester Counties. The monitoring function was important and our obligation to enforce implementation was the heart and soul of our mission.

The Panel initially determined that its approach should be non-adversarial. We felt that a spirit of cooperation would be most beneficial, since both the Judge and Governor Carey placed their support of, and devotion to, full implementation. The representatives of the plaintiffs and the representatives of the defense, two sides who had been embroiled in a three-year courtroom battle, would work together in a spirit of harmony and sharing.

Right.

Unfortunately, it quickly became apparent that the defendants were approaching the Willowbrook Consent Judgment as a nuisance and the Willowbrook Review Panel as a cluster of substitute teachers to be controlled, undermined, manipulated or disregarded. Rather than seeking to learn how we could best implement the provisions of the Consent Judgment, the Department of Mental Hygiene seemed determined to maintain the *status quo* by doing as little as possible, while avoiding charges of contempt. Our approach, as provided in the Consent Judgment, was to fully implement the provisions, while the State always sought to minimize implementation of the provisions and to delay even that. Invariably the State rejected our formal recommendations, and sought additional time to perform any action or provide any reports or records. The State's efforts were aimed at simply delaying everything until we got tired and it could go back to its usual process without intrusions.

We seemed to always be speaking at cross-purposes with the State representatives. They pressed to marginally improve the conditions of the institutions, move residents from one institution to another, to reduce the population of Willowbrook, and pay no meaningful attention to community placement and the development of community services.

Schools, medical and therapeutic support services, day and vocational services and , of course, residential facilities, needed to be created but the bulk of the funds the State was willing to provide was to improve the institutions but not to support community placements.

At one point, Mike and I were so exasperated that we got up and left the conference room. We stood in the hall and I said, "this is ridiculous. They agreed to the terms. Ordered by a federal judge."

"Judge isn't here," Michael said.

"Gentlemen?" One of the defendants' representatives peeked out into the hallway with a suspiciously friendly smile. "Come on back in!"

We reentered, and took our spot at the table, opposite the representatives of the state. They began.

"You've heard of Exodus, right?" They gestured to me. "Well, *you've* heard of it."

"Yes, thank you. The liberation of the Israelite slaves from Egypt."

"Right!"

I can't wait to hear this, I thought to myself.

"So the plan we've come up with, and we think is a great solution, is this: we empty Willowbrook completely."

Jim said, "so far, so good."

"We take state funds to rehabilitate wards in existing institutions. The wards will be like new! Everyone gets a fresh start. Willowbrook is closed and everybody's happy!"

Somewhere, an angel screamed.

Mike Lottman asked, "what existing institutions?"

They smiled. "We have that information somewhere." Considering they had done the opening presentation without a glance at a page, they took their time sorting through pages to find the answer to that one. "Here it is: Glen Oaks at Creedmoor a new unit of Fineson, Brooklyn, Manhattan, and…."

Like all public institutions, each one had a reputation worse than the one before.

Linda Glenn's face went white. "What about community placement?" she demanded.

Mike Lottman spoke up. "So this plan—and I'm using the word 'plan' loosely'—you two didn't come up with it on your own?"

"No," they offered."

"Of course not."

I chimed in. "Any idea how much this fiasco would cost?"

"We can bring it in at under $50 million."

"50 million?" I was about to let loose a tirade, thought how it might affect Lara and the other residents, and took a breath. "I have a better idea. What if you take the same 50 million dollars and use it to implement the community placement plan that is already in the judgment you agreed to?"

"I'm sorry. We don't have the authority to do that."

That's how it went. The State believed that, if Willowbrook could be emptied, all problems, pressures and criticisms would disappear and the institutional system would survive. Why did the institutional system need to survive? Because it brought in money through the established process and it had always been done that way.

The use of the term "Exodus" horrified me. Would it be liberation to be transferred from Willowbrook to the Glen Oaks Unit in Creedmoor, or to Brooklyn, or to Suffolk, or any other institution? Creedmoor was a mental institution and the State transferred mentally retarded individuals from Willowbrook to the two top floors, of Creedmoor. The Department of Mental Hygiene smiled down on us with its reassurance that things would now be different, things would finally change, and that community services would be immediately forthcoming, as its new and principal emphasis. This was not just wishful thinking but a ridiculous fantasy.

Moreover, something was basically wrong. The smiles were sweet but the numbers were sour. No one who is serious or sane would spend $50 million to rehabilitate old, temporary, inappropriate buildings, in order to "prepare" the institutionalized residents for placement into community residences. Linda Glenn made it clear that no retarded person required "preparation" to move to community placement. It would have made more sense for the State to recommend allocations of $2 million to clean up and maintain the institutions for the residents, until they could be placed into the community, and $50 million for the development of permanent community residential facilities. I guess such "sense" was not in their budget. Nevertheless, the State officials were unwilling to budge.

I also recall the Department of Mental Hygiene's use of the term "decompression." This term referred to the State's plan to transfer residents from Willowbrook to other institutions, in order to reduce the number of residents living in Willowbrook. Such transfers would reduce the overcrowded conditions existing in the Willowbrook buildings, thereby reducing the population and "decompressing" the residents. These artificial terms were used to camouflage the sad and sorry truth of unhealthy overcrowding. While the reduction of overcrowding is a benefit, it would delay the ultimate benefit of community placement. It was our belief that earlier placement trumped earlier reduction of overcrowding. At the same time, each placement reduced overcrowding.

"Exodus" was ready for implementation. The Panel had to act quickly and issued a formal recommendation seeking to halt the planned transfer of Class Members to other institutions. The formal recommendation issued by the Review Panel required that all Class Members be placed from Willowbrook, or related institutions, directly into community residential programs. No lateral transfer from institution to institution or retention of residents in the institution was to be permitted for a Class Member, unless and until the Department of Mental Hygiene could establish to the Review Panel that such transfer or retention would be the least restrictive environment possible for each such individual. We had previously established that the term "possible" was defined as "required and appropriate" not merely "available." And any determination that the institution was appropriate, had to be supported with adequate documentation. Not surprisingly, Commissioner Kolb rejected this formal recommendation.

To slow things down even more, Commissioner Kolb refused to provide the Willowbrook Review Panel with copies of relevant records we requested. He cited "confidentiality" as the basis for refusing to provide us with records.

I responded to his office. "The State voluntarily negotiated and agreed to the Willowbrook Consent Judgment. You already agreed and the judgment provides the right of access to records of the residents."

The message came back with a frazzled secretary reading his response: "Commissioner Kolb insists that you're not entitled to records based upon…the requirements of confidentiality, and rejects your recommendation interpreting the Consent Judgment as allowing full access of all records to the Panel."

Such was the State game plan. Refuse to comply with what it had already agreed to do. Ultimately, we prevailed but it set the tone and the adversarial relationship was cemented. There was no meeting them halfway.

When I became a member of the Willowbrook Review Panel and got to know the other plaintiffs' members, I realized that I was home. Finally, I was with a group of smart, caring, knowledgeable individuals who I could work with, specifically Jim Clements, Mike Lottman and Linda Glenn. More importantly, I knew I could almost always rely on a four-vote majority on all important issues. At first, the votes were unanimous. As we reached deeper, more and more of the defendants' designees voted "no." Such votes did not upset or concern me. I deemed every affirmative vote from a member selected by the defendants to be a gift.

Bill Bitner selected by the defendants and serving as an Assistant Commissioner for the State Education Department, was a knowledgeable, independent member who voted his beliefs and never manifested that he was acting on behalf of the defendants. Nevertheless, Bill was the product the State Education Department, so he was reluctant to attack the higher-ups. Bill was very orderly and believed in respecting organizational plans. If the benefits of the Willowbrook Consent Judgment were to benefit mentally retarded people in the State of New York, the system had to change. Perhaps the Willowbrook Consent Judgment was never able or meant to sweep so far and deeply. But this was the only broom we had. To me, it was not possible to correct the manner of delivering proper services to the mentally retarded without changing the current system.

I used to compare Willowbrook and other institutions for the mentally retarded, with Auschwitz, Bergen-Belsen, and other concentration camps. The obvious distinction is that concentration camps had the stated goal of killing the inmates, while that was not the stated goal of Willowbrook and its kind. But both Willowbrook and Auschwitz had captive inhabitants. Willowbrook had forced residents through a lack of alternatives. Both populations had to endure deplorable living conditions and neither facility supported life. Willowbrook failed to support life in that it failed to assure that the residents would thrive. Its mentally retarded population was merely to remain there until each person died.

But every person needs the opportunity to live in a home without the fear of neglect and deplorable conditions. Such failure is akin to slaughtering the mentally retarded in a slow, horrific process. Through understaffing and neglect, Willowbrook followed a process that resulted in premature death. While nursing homes for the aged have been referred to being "G-d's waiting rooms," the same may be said for institutions for the mentally retarded.

When the State identified the most fragile, poor black and Puerto Rican inhabitants at Willowbrook and transferred them to Gouverneur Hospital, did they intend to kill those children? Probably not, but they made no meaningful efforts to see to it that they would thrive and live the best life they could. The state actually selected those children to be moved to a hospital where the care was alleged to be even worse than that at Willowbrook. My remarkable friend, Goody, with her will of steel, fouled up the State's plan.

We already established that there is no economy of size. If anything, large institutions for the mentally retarded are more expensive to operate than are small residential residences. Moreover, the cost of institutions in human terms is incalculable. Residents are subjected to lives of isolation and deprivation. Moving them to a newer, cleaner holding tank was not going to change that.

26

A GOAL ACCOMPLISHED

On April 1, 1979, eleven years after Lara's admission to Willowbrook, following many years of dreams and plans, battles and skirmishes, and even some negotiating, the first apartment for profoundly retarded multiply handicapped children in the State of New York opened in Bayside, Queens. And, even more importantly, it was Lara's new home to be shared with three other lucky children. The apartment opened without much public fanfare but with our own private celebration. Four profoundly retarded multiply handicapped children would share a home in a regular apartment house, on a regular block, in a regular neighborhood. Their new home would be walking distance to a shopping center with stores, a Waldbaum's super market, a Chinese restaurant, a pizzeria, doctors, dentists, public buses, you name it, it was right there.

Since the apartment was the children's home, it was furnished for their comfort and benefit. The children were non-ambulatory and suffered from spasticity and contractures, so the furniture mostly consisted of beanbag seats, bolsters, large mats and plush carpet. Just a few regular chairs, two rocking chairs to sit with the children, and one small sofa were available for guests and staff. Each child had their own clothes, toys, decorations for their bedroom, photos and stereos, and soft, calming music was played almost constantly. In addition, each child had their own personalized wheelchair, adapted to each child's physical limitations and needs.

From the moment Lara moved into the apartment she became a very busy girl. She began going to school a full day, Monday through Friday. The children were picked up in specially equipped vans before 9:00 a.m. and retuned home about 3:00 p.m. During the school day Lara was exposed to other children, the normal sounds of a school, was given physical therapy to reduce her spasticity and contractures, and was given speech therapy to help her with swallowing. A notebook containing messages and recommendations accompanied each child that was exchanged between the school therapists and the apartment staff so that the staff would be kept up to date about the child's programs and progress. They all made specific efforts to treat Lara, and each child, as a valuable individual.

The apartment staff was composed of loving, committed people who cared deeply about others and embraced our concepts of "normalization," the right of every person to live in a loving home. They considered it part of their job to make the apartment a real home for the children and it was easy to see that they took great pride in their success. I could see that each child knew or sensed that she was loved and cared for, even cherished. I noticed that, in spite of the fact that Lara was profoundly retarded and blind, she seemed to pay attention to a person who spoke directly to her. She would attempt to face the speaker and would remain quiet.

Lara and her apartment mates were kept busy on the weekends as well. They were taken to various community functions and had trips to parks, museums, plays, amusement parks, restaurants and the like. This was "normalization" at its best. Although I was delighted that she had so many activities, it also reduced my time with her. It felt odd that my profoundly retarded multiply handicapped daughter was too busy for some long weekends at our home. Surely, the parents of the children formerly warehoused at Willowbrook would think me mad.

Best of all, Lara's apartment was just a few blocks from our home. Although she did not live with us under the same roof, she was close to us and it was easy to see her at almost any time. We had worked hard for this and we reached an amazing success. Certainly any parent with a profoundly retarded child would be thrilled with a similar situation but, somehow, I was unable to truly rejoice. The realization that joy and pain live in the same heart and at the same time was uncomfortable and difficult to reconcile. It was the goal we had fought for but it was oddly disconcerting. In retrospect, I believe my conflict related to the fact that, although Lara was in the best possible situation she could be in, I could never have what I *really* wanted, a fully whole Lara.

27

BAT MITZVAH

Sweet Lara turned 13 years old on May 23, 1981. That I had three other beautiful red-haired children did not reduce her shine. She remained as sweet and beautiful as she was at the age of one. There was no change in her at all, except that she got older and slightly larger. She never grew to be four feet long (I use the word "long," a measure used for babies, rather than "tall," a measure used for children who can stand unassisted) and she never weighed more than 40 pounds. She never was able to sit, stand or walk. She was an infant in all respects, dependent upon full time services for every function and for survival itself. But as puberty approached she began to develop breasts and pubic hair. This was very uncomfortable and disconcerting for me.

The inability to communicate with Lara could be very painful. I could not say, "Today is Sunday. I'll be back on Monday," or any other day, and expect her to understand. So most of my visits at her apartment or at home involved holding, kissing, rocking, walking, and singing. She seemed happy and peaceful in my arms, and I felt the same way.

As always, when I ran out of lullabies, I switched to Frank Sinatra songs. Sooner or later, I would get to "I See Your Face Before Me" with its beautiful haunting lyrics. I would sing sadly and longingly.

> *It doesn't matter where you are*
> *I can see how fair you are.*

I had long stopped running down the corridor hopefully anticipating some change, any change, as it was clear that Lara was exactly who she was and who she would always be. I never played the mental game of trying to put her beautiful face on a normal body. Yet, I always happily anticipated every visit. The sadness was part of my life but so was the love.

Her sisters and brother, Elizabeth, Samantha and Joshua, loved Lara and stuck by her. At least once this paid off. One day, we all went to a small one-ring circus. We parked, placed Lara into her wheelchair and headed for the entrance. As we entered, a manager escorted us into the tent but not to our ticketed seats. Instead, he took us to the front edge of the ring. Elizabeth, Samantha and Josh were delighted and impressed. Their big sister was a celebrity.

They were very caring toward her. They checked her from head to toe for bruises, scrapes, irregularities, when she arrived at the house and before she was returned to wherever she was staying. They flitted in and out of whatever room she was in, to be sure that she was not alone. They adjusted to who Lara was and never seemed embarrassed by being in public with her.

As we approached Lara's 13th birthday, Vicki and I had decided that, as a Jewish girl, she should have a Bat Mitzvah ceremony. Most Jewish 13 year old boys attend a rite called a Bar Mitzvah and many 13 year old girls attend a Bat Mitzvah. Such rites are somewhat similar to a confirmation. We met with our religious leader, Rabbi Hyman Levine, and informed him of our plans. He was familiar with the work we were doing for the mentally retarded and had become a social worker providing services to the mentally retarded. Although he was happy and honored to conduct the service, he faced a problem with his Ritual Committee. The Committee opposed a Bat Mitzvah for Lara because she did not have the mental capacity to actively participate in the ritual. She could not recite the ritual prayers. Rabbi Levine short-circuited the opposition by informing them that he supported the Schneps' efforts, and further, "Mr. Schneps is a litigator for the handicapped, and a suit would be rained upon us." I never uttered words or threats of that kind to Rabbi Levine, but he had his own methods and the Bat Mitzvah was approved.

At the service, in the presence of all in attendance, I stated:

> Society has not, as yet, overcome its belief that the mentally handicapped are not equal before G-d. The word of G-d which commands that all of His children are equal before him – whether or not they can perform His words – is systematically disregarded.

Recently Vicki, Elizabeth and I saw "Children of A Lesser G-d," a play with deaf characters. The play is wonderful but the title creates a wrongful impression. There is no different or lesser G-d for the handicapped. G-d must not be judged by the acts of man. There are only lesser people and lesser people are not those who are handicapped in their ability to learn and walk. Lesser people are those who lack generosity of thought and action toward others.

Just because one cannot chew does not mean he or she should not be fed.

Just because one cannot walk does not mean that he or she should not be taken.

Just because one cannot ask does not mean that he or she should not receive.

Not everyone got the message.

28

FORMAL RECOMMENDATIONS

The Willowbrook Review Panel made its best progress and secured the best changes through the Formal Recommendation process. While some of the State employees, including the Commissioner, Assistant Commissioners, and other administrators, gave some assistance in complying with the Consent Judgment, it was the persistence of some parents and the action of the Willowbrook Review Panel that made real progress a possibility.

The Willowbrook Review Panel issued 22 formal recommendations. Our goal was to place as many people in community residences as we could. The recommendations were generally reactions to situations and needs that came to our attention. More like plugging the holes in a dike than building from a foundation.

I argued that all community residential facilities for the mentally retarded should have but three beds each. That goal is rarely achieved. I knew that community residential programs should never be operated by the State. Voluntary agencies should develop and operate community residential programs, with the State providing funding and oversight assuring high quality services and providing expert assistance and guidance. Additionally, I envisioned that a large number of small voluntary agencies should be developed and organized to operate small community residential programs. No agency should become large, lest it become too dominant and too powerful. When the large agencies are too powerful and influential, the operation becomes infested with politics, which reduces its ability to fulfill its major responsibility of providing direct services and coordination.

In spite of our successes, we were involved in a critical race. When would our oversight end? Obviously, the State understood that fact as well. However, it knew that it would survive forever and it played its hand accordingly. The State rejected formal recommendation after formal recommendation, causing a great deal of busy work for the panel. I was trying to keep my law office operating. Thankfully, Mike handled much more of the paperwork than I did. Although our recommendations carried great weight, we still had to answer each challenge, prepare for and conduct each hearing. And we were part-timers. The State worked full-time.

Our other formal recommendations included various actions to improve conditions for the class members. None of them were seriously rejected by the Court. However, the class members were forced to endure delays upon delays. Even simple things that the Panel assumed was not debatable, like not using physical restraints without documented need, was met with resistance and created great amounts of busy work.

We spent extensive time and effort in accomplishing basic reforms and responding to emergencies. These included closing the Keener Unit, a small residential institution that became contaminated with carbon monoxide; securing access to resident records for the Panel and the parents; halting the firing of teachers and reinstating the residents back into their education programs; closing the so-called "Behavior Modification Unit" and the horrific "Psychiatric Unit" where residents got worse and worse; securing the hiring of a competent medical director; providing adequate clothing; preventing the full utilization of the Bronx Developmental Center (see, Chapter 29); closing the Hillcrest Unit (see Chapter 30) where young men were wrongfully and improperly imprisoned; hiring additional staff; and the eventual closing of the Gouverneur Hospital. Of course, our most meaningful accomplishment was the design and implementation of the Community Placement Plan, an accomplishment extensively participated with Barbara Blum, head of the Metropolitan Placement Unit (MPU), Dr. Jennifer House, our executive director, and a seemingly army of experts.

While it is true that I had fought to prevent the closing of Gouverneur, that was at a time when community placement was difficult or unavailable and they were to be sent back to Willowbrook. As that changed, moving the residents and closing Gouverneur was an appropriate goal.

Many of Gouverneur's former residents, now adults happily reside in apartments in Manhattan, in conditions as normal as are possible. Margaret, the daughter of protest organizer Willie Mae Goodman ("Goody"), continues to live in an apartment several blocks from Goody's apartment.

Nothing was easy with the State. The Panel even had to spend precious time and energy to get the State to accept a reasonable definition of the word "children."

Somehow, the State insisted that childhood ended at 16 years of age. New York State law mandates a free education to every person up to the age of 21years.

The formal recommendations were extensive and wide reaching. Without the formal recommendation process, little would have been accomplished.

29

BRONX DEVELOPMENTAL CENTER

One pet program of mine was seeking to prevent the use of the newly constructed but, as yet, unopened house of horrors known as the Bronx Developmental Center. Following my visit to the recently completed institution, I became determined to prevent its utilization as a residential facility for the mentally retarded. Many Willowbrook Class Members were scheduled to be transferred to the Bronx Developmental Center. It was the State's plan to construct and open institutions in each of the five New York City counties. It already had four of the counties covered: Willowbrook in Staten Island (Richmond County), Manhattan Developmental Center (New York County), Brooklyn Developmental Center (Kings County) and Bernard Fineson Developmental Center (Queens County). The Bronx Developmental Center (Bronx County) would complete the set, the fifth "jewel" in the crown.

But "jewel" is not the right word.

Even using the most lax standards, the Bronx Developmental Center was wholly inappropriate as a residential facility for the mentally retarded. It had a sleek nautical design that, at first glance, would have made a dandy dormitory for a naval academy. The profile was that of a large ship and most of the exterior was covered with stainless steel. Internally, its stairs, hallways, railings and windows mimicked the insides of a ship. The stairs were constructed with open lattice-work gratings and had no risers to prevent a foot from slipping through. Many hallways contained wide-spaced pipe railings to protect against open floors below. The pipe railings ran horizontally two feet apart and would easily permit someone to fall or climb between them and fall to the floor below. Each bedroom contained round windows resembling ship portholes and one or two oblong windows installed an inch or two above the floor. I was shocked.

"Okay, I give up," I said to my guide. "What's with the windows at floor level?"

"Oh! The architect, Richard Meier, visited Willowbrook. He noticed that lots of the mentally retarded people there were sitting or lying on the floor, so…"

"So he put the windows there."

"Exactly!"

The architect had concluded that severely and profoundly retarded people *liked* to sit and lie on the floor. Apparently, he did not notice that there was nothing else in the ward to sit on. I thought of asking if he planned to pre-smear the floors with feces, knowing how happy that seemed to make the residents.

The new Bronx Developmental Center had to be rejected but there would be a battle. The building had been planned, constructed, and paid for over a period of years and it was an essential part of the Department of Mental Hygiene's overall plans. Moreover, it cost the taxpayers the staggering sum of $25 million. Still, the Panel agreed to take some action, and I was authorized to draft a letter to Commissioner Kolb expressing "our concern over the planned opening" of the new institutional facility and asking Dr. Kolb to "reconsider this decision" and, also, to issue directions "terminating such plans, so that the Bronx Developmental Center would never be utilized, even temporarily, as a residential institution for the mentally retarded." We noted in our letter that the State's plans for the Bronx Developmental Center building pre-dated the issuance of the Willowbrook Review Panel's Community Placement Plan, and it was clear that money required for the opening and maintaining of the institution would tap funds from, and negatively affect, the community placement efforts. My letter made it clear to Dr. Kolb that the letter was not a formal recommendation but was "merely a request and suggestion by the Review Panel" and it sought a written response or, at minimum, a discussion of the matter.

Dr. Kolb wrote back. Jim Clements read his letter aloud to the panel. "The logical extension of your request would be to stop all admissions to all State facilities in the State....My decision is to proceed according to plan."

Mike Lottman said, "He won't even *discuss* it?"

Linda Glenn said, "Well, that's so dismissive!"

Every review panel member agreed.

"That's an insult."

I smiled to myself. The panel was ready for action.

There is always the threat, even the likelihood, that the new boss will be worse than the old boss. But that fear, that "better the devil you know" attitude, keeps people at horrible jobs and reelecting horrible leaders, year after year.

I said, "How many in this room have had enough of Commissioner Kolb?"

Reputedly, Dr. Kolb was a fine psychiatrist. He was the head of a small psychiatric unit in Manhattan. As Commissioner, he was out of his depth. A psychiatrist is a healer. A Commissioner is an executive, an administrator who must attend to the needs of the Governor. So many, if not all, of the issues are political. Dr. Kolb had neither experience nor skill in politics. He failed to know how to communicate with us or anticipate our actions. Even worse he had neither expertise in mental retardation nor knowledge of the culture in the Department of Mental Hygiene. We informed Chris Hansen that we were unwilling to continue to deal with Dr. Kolb and sought his removal from authority in all matters relating to the Willowbrook Consent Judgment and the Willowbrook Review Panel. If he was not removed from the case, we were prepared to take the matter to Judge Bartels. Chris Hansen transmitted our dissatisfaction with

Dr. Kolb to the State's lawyers, the Office of Attorney General Louis Lefkowitz.

Our efforts were successful.

Commissioner Kolb issued Commissioner Memorandum No. 113 delegating "all necessary authority and operational responsibility for implementation of the Willowbrook Consent Decree in the office of the Deputy Commissioner for Mental Retardation" to Tom Coughlin. While we were able to finesse the removal of Dr. Kolb from operational responsibility regarding the Willowbrook Consent Judgment, Dr. Kolb continued to be the Commissioner. This made us happy. While it is true that we frequently argued and wrestled with Tom, we all respected him. Prior to his appointment as commissioner, Tom had been a strong and vigorous advocate for the mentally retarded operating an agency in Watertown, New York and was a New York State trooper. But now his job was that of a political and financial manager. Advocacy was not part of his job description. But he never forgot where he came from.

So we still had to stop the Bronx Developmental Center from opening. We had not struggled so long to save the kids at Willowbrook just to move them into a newer, scarier hell and even further from any semblance of a home. The Panel issued a formal recommendation stating, "That the Bronx Developmental Center not be utilized as a residential facility for members of the Willowbrook class." This was a remarkable achievement because many of the Review Panel members were reluctant to prevent the State from utilizing a brand new facility that cost 25 million dollars. A vote for the formal recommendation was a major affront to the Governor, the Legislature and, especially, to Commissioner Kolb.

The case went to trial. Judge John R. Bartels presided over the United States District Court in Brooklyn.

But the State questioned the legal authority of the Review Panel to recommend that Willowbrook class members not be transferred to the Bronx Developmental Center, relying upon Judge Judd's earlier decision permitting some interim transfers from Willowbrook to other institutions, and argued the merits of the new unused building. Needless to say, we won.

The plaintiffs and the Willowbrook Review Panel argued that the new Bronx Developmental Center was an unfortunate venture that should not be opened or used for any Willowbrook Class Members. We based our arguments on both the failings of the building itself and to the harm to class members being transferred to a further institution rather than immediate placement in community residential programs.

Judge Bartels confirmed the formal recommendation and rejected the State's opposition. "The court is concerned about the deleterious effect the transfers to the Bronx Developmental Center of Willowbrook class members might have on their community placement in the future," he said. "Therefore, the court is convinced that transfers to the Bronx Developmental Center will create a risk of loss of present improvement and also of delay in community placement, where the only real improvement in the handicapped and retarded can be expected." In an effort to soften the blow of some parents who were anxious to move their children into the Bronx where they resided adding, "Nothing in this opinion, however, shall prevent the Department from considering a transfer of a resident requested by a parent or guardian and transferring said resident to the Bronx Developmental Center in accordance with such request and established procedures." He was a wise man.

I knew what I thought of residents being moved on a "transitional basis." It was expensive, pointless and mostly permanent.

Few, if any, Class members were transferred from Willowbrook to the Bronx Developmental Center, and the Bronx Developmental Center's life as a residential institution was short-lived. From the first moment I set my eyes upon that facility, I imagined my Lara being forced to live in such an inappropriate residential institution. It was beyond scary. It was ridiculous and obscene. My Lara would never live in that place and I took every step I could to prevent any mentally retarded person from being forced to live there.

30

THE HILLCREST UNIT

Jim Clements and I determined that it was necessary for us to visit each institution where Class Members resided. On August 13, 1976, we visited the Wingdale Unit of the Wassaic Developmental Center in upstate New York where some Willowbrook class members resided in ugly brick buildings surrounded by a beautiful landscape of grass and trees. During our visit we learned of the existence of a smaller unit within Wingdale known as Hillcrest, a former private school, housing young men in prisonlike circumstances. The young men, gathered from the upstate area, were deemed to be dangerous or difficult to manage.

Jim and I secured directions and immediately drove to the Hillcrest Unit. We found a small prison for 18 young men, mostly in their 20s, eight of them Willowbrook class members entitled to the benefits of the Willowbrook Consent Judgment. These were our guys. The young men were imprisoned in a building located in an isolated area in the woods. A narrow road connected the main road to the building. It was surrounded by trees and overgrown shrubs and only became visible as you drew closer. The location offered complete privacy and seclusion, begging the question of why housing for the mentally retarded would require such isolation.

The supervisor met us when we entered. He told us that these young men were aggressive, difficult to deal with and had a tendency to run away from their former institutions.

Every window and door was locked, so the young men had no freedom to roam anywhere but inside the building. We were granted access to the files and determined that none of the young men had ever been arrested or convicted of any crime. Their primary misbehavior appeared to be running away from their former institutions. They were confined by the State, nonetheless. Frankly, to me, their tendency to run away was more of a sign of intelligence than a basis for punishment.

Jim and I spoke to each young man individually and in small groups.

Although they were limited by their institutional deprivations, they did not appear to be mentally retarded. Neither Jim nor I, nor later on Linda Glenn, thought they were retarded, with one exception.

Jim, being a physician, determined that the men were subjected to the overuse of psychotropic drugs *PRN.* "PRN" means, "as needed." The staff could administer psychotropic drugs to any person at whim. According to Jim's assessment all but one of the young men was suitable for immediate placement in a small residential facility, with limited supervision. Linda and I, and other Panel members, later confirmed his findings.

Discussions of the situation were held on the next day, at the next regular meeting of the Panel. Jim Forde, Regional Director of the Department of Mental Hygiene and Thomas Coughlin, Deputy Commissioner, were both present. The Panel members were shocked by our reports.

Jim Forde seemed uncomfortable. "Jim and Murray, I am shocked. I never knew this place existed. I am so embarrassed. What can we do? I will visit myself on Monday," he promised. While I liked Jim Forde, the barrel was aimed at his head. This was his region and he was the Regional Director.

Tom Coughlin was similarly embarrassed. "Everything will be done to right this situation," he said, and also promised to visit the Hillcrest Unit.

Jim Forde called me Monday morning. "I just saw Hillcrest," he said.

"Did I exaggerate?"

"No," he groaned. "It's all true." He hung up.

The panel issued a formal recommendation immediately. This was an emergency situation.

We recommended that the eight young men who were from Willowbrook be removed from the Hillcrest Unit and placed in individually appropriate facilities with suitable programs and that the Hillcrest Unit would not be utilized for any other Members of the Willowbrook Class, without prior consultation with and express written consent and approval of the Panel. We also urged that the Hillcrest Unit should not be utilized for housing anyone, regardless of his or her membership in the Willowbrook Class.

Not surprisingly, Commissioner Kolb denied our requests and objected to the Formal Recommendation. Rather than accepting the formal recommendation Commissioner Kolb played for time and delayed. He offered consolation saying, "As you know from the phone conversations with Mr. Forde and Mr. Coughlin, the Department shares your concern with the program at Hillcrest." He then offered us an assessment process and the appointment of an expert from the American Correctional Association who was in the Retarded Correctional Association. I was fuming. These young men were incarcerated without the benefit of charges or a judge or jury. We confirmed the evaluation that all but one of these men could function well in community residences.

The Review Panel wanted to avoid another legal confrontation and sought to resolve the matter by getting appropriate services to the young men. We made more visits to the Hillcrest Unit and issued a second Formal Recommendation. The Panel recommended that the State provide detailed written plans for the moving the eight class members from the Hillcrest Unit to appropriate community residential programs, with necessary support services, within 90 days. We made specific detailed prescriptions for seven class members, who could immediately be placed in the community. For the eighth class member, who required special services, we sought additional programs in a community residence, including speech therapy, behavior modification, and participation in planning for placement in the community. He was a rather large young man, perhaps, 6'4", 285 pounds, whose size seemed to scare everyone. Finally, the Commissioner agreed. Perhaps he felt he had stalled long enough.

I was driven by a single principle: every retarded person should be cared for in circumstances that addressed his particular needs. The same care I wanted for Lara.

We won another round. And all we had to do was prove that eighteen young men had been confined and over medicated because someone thought that they could be difficult to deal with.

31

TRUTH TELLING

In dealing with the requirements of the Willowbrook Consent Judgment and the Community Placement Plan, the State brought in its mental retardation administrators to lead, or in my view obstruct, its side of the operation. The Office of Mental Retardation and Developmental Disabilities (OMRDD - the new name for the Department of Mental Hygiene) formed a New York City Metropolitan Placement Unit (MPU). OMRDD named Barbara Blum to be the head of the MPU. Barbara was a lovely, able and highly competent person. The fact that she had a handicapped child did not hurt. Barbara's deputy was Michael Mascari, a former New York City Assistant Commissioner for Mental Retardation. I liked Mike but I, initially, thought he was too soft for the job. The key was developing group homes and a group home system. Such a system required the acquisition and the arrangement of many services, including: educational, medical, social, habilitation, rehabilitation, and others.

I was wrong about Mike. He did an excellent job and, under Barbara Blum, was generating and creating high-level community placements, at a very fast rate. And most importantly, the placements were excellent in terms of services and operations. People who had merely survived in Willowbrook, and other New York City and New York State institutions, were now living good, safe, fulfilling, and enjoyable lives. The Panel was very satisfied with Mike's work and was elated with his demonstrated skills, commitment, and strength. Mike was helping to make the Community Placement Plan work. People who formerly sat around in idleness, awaiting death, now lived in real homes, which were alive with the sounds, smells, and senses of life and the living.

So the State "fired" him.

The firing took the form of a transfer to a new position in Albany. He had done too well, made too much progress, expanded too many community placements. They decided to send him off with a celebratory luncheon. He called me.

"They're throwing me a catered lynching."

"Luncheon."

"Semantics. Want to say a few words? Think of it as a pre-eulogy."

I got to the catering hall, speech in hand, and found Mike. Some well-wisher was pumping his arm. Mike looked green at the gills. He turned to me.

"Thank God," he said, though we had not been such great friends. "I don't know how much more of this I can take."

"Of what?"

He scanned the room. "Listen, you're up last. Just do your usual thing and don't worry about being polite."

And he walked off.

I took my place on the dais as the speeches began.

"Mike Mascari is a terrific guy…" True.

"About the sweetest guy you could ever know…" Also true.

"New York's loss is Albany's gain." True, but not the point.

"Great at his job…" Way too true.

Mike was being shipped out of town, involuntarily "transferred" from New York City to Albany, for being too good at a job that the State never wanted to see done at all. It was suddenly so obvious. Also obvious was that he wanted someone to speak on his behalf by telling the unwashed truth. And he knew the exact right person up to the task. He did not ask me to speak because we were such great friends, or because I was such a nice guy, but because he trusted me. I was the truth teller.

He had not let us down. I was not about to let him down.

Lara was living in an apartment, receiving the services she required. I refused to celebrate Mike's removal or make believe this was not a step backwards.

I scanned my notes: a terrific guy . . . a sweet guy. . . New York City's loss . . .

I decided to proceed extemporaneously.

When it was my turn, I took the podium. I looked out over a sea of painted-on smiles and addressed many executive directors of voluntary agencies who were opening and maintaining group homes.

"I cannot share your enthusiasm with Michael's so-called 'promotion.' This is not a promotion but rather a beheading. Beware: soon all your heads will be chopped off. Mike was dumped because he was doing a great job in placing people into the community. And his removal will make it more difficult for you to get adequate funding to expand your placement efforts."

Some in the audience gasped, some twisted their faces into smirks, some smiled. I went on.

"It is time to wake up and realize that we are in the midst of a war, a war to protect the mentally retarded we are devoted to serve. Without Mike, it will be more difficult to move forward and accomplish our goals. The battlefield is in New York City, not in Albany. Mike will now be in Albany. Get the picture?" I snarled. "In closing... Mike. I apologize. At first, I thought you weren't up for the job. I couldn't have been more wrong. You handled your job perfectly. Too perfectly to be left to complete it."

Following my words several people came up to me to thank me for speaking the truth. Most puzzling were the words from Dr. Bernard Tesse the Director of the Bernard Fineson Developmental Center, in Queens. Dr. Tesse shook my hand with energy and said, in his heavy accent, "Mr. Schneps, dat is exactly vat I said."

Huh? Where? When? I had no idea what he thought he had said. Then he offered, "You are da fadder ov

Villowbrook." Of course, even a charlatan may speak some truth.

Dr. Tesse was amazingly manipulative. He knew and frequently dealt with Vicki, who served as President of the Bernard Fineson Board of Visitors. On one occasion he told her, "Yer huzbant haz converted antisocial behavior into a force ov good." Another time he volunteered to Vicki with reference to me, "I am concerned how a person who hates zo mach can luff?"

Of course, in a world with killers and victims, I have chosen to love the lambs.

Oh, lest I forget to mention it, Dr. Tesse was a psychiatrist.

32

CEREBRAL PALSY

At home everything was about the same except for one additional piece of information - Lara had cerebral palsy.

My Lara was multiply handicapped, profoundly retarded, blind and also suffered from cerebral palsy. Even though I had the ability and desire to acquire information on almost any subject, it took me several years to learn this fact. None of our phalanx of physicians, not our original pediatrician, our pediatric neurologist, our next pediatrician, or our consultant pediatric neurologist, ever suggested cerebral palsy. Basically, they assumed we knew. No physician ever directly informed me of Lara's cerebral palsy. Perhaps to them it was so obvious. Not to me!

One day, I asked a physician if Lara's spasticity was related to her brain damage and was told that she suffered from cerebral palsy. It was frustrating to experience how reluctant even great professionals could be with sharing *all* the information with the parents of handicapped children.

I had watched, year after year, the United Cerebral Palsy Telethon. During those sad, uplifting, glorious, visual and editorial telethons I never saw, and they never presented, a child similar to Lara. The children with cerebral palsy displayed on the show were all normal except that they suffered from cerebral palsy. They never displayed or mentioned the existence of a cerebral palsied mentally retarded child. Surprise, surprise! I guess a profoundly mentally retarded, cerebral palsied child is not commercially viable.

Knowing that Lara had cerebral palsy did not unnerve me, nothing changed. If anything, it gave me peace to put a name on some of her symptoms. Lara was still Lara and I still raised my children as I always had and my office was still in Manhattan. You get into a rhythm of life and continue to live. Lara had three siblings and two parents who loved her with all their hearts. I liked to think that this was part of the set-up in life, that even someone like Lara, born with the cards stacked against her, at least gets a loving family. Of course, that was not true for everyone.

I met one person for whom that was not true. Bernard Carabello had been admitted to Willowbrook in 1953, when he was three years old. It is not difficult to believe that his parents were told, like so many parents, that placing Bernard was the only option for their mentally retarded son. The problem with that advice was that Bernard was *not* mentally retarded. He had difficulty speaking and walking because he had cerebral palsy. Apparently, no tests or diagnostic examinations were ever conducted and he later contracted polio at Willowbrook. So much for it being the best place for Bernard to receive care and treatment.

It was obvious to the staff that Bernard was bright and inquisitive. Too bad his family did not visit regularly. Perhaps they would have seen his progress and helped him escape, or perhaps that was my fantasy. Despite the fact that he received no family support, no schooling and no training, he grew into a compassionate and generous young man. When I first met him, he was a teenager working around the various offices and had been befriended by Dr. Mike Wilkins and Elizabeth Lee.

Years later I learned that his obvious intelligence made him an unwilling worker on the understaffed wards. He was forced to mop and wash the floors, collect and sort the laundry, and to bath, clean, and toilet his fellow residents. He was rewarded with peanut butter sandwiches or cigarettes, despite the fact that he did not smoke. More troubling was the fact that, if he did not perform his assigned task in a timely manner, he would be denied privileges or, worse, beaten. How do you abuse a young person with cerebral palsy and polio for not doing unpaid work quickly enough? That's not a question I could answer nor could I answer how a child who had no nurturing, no support system, and none of the advantages we take for granted, could grow into a generous and loving man. But it happened. If I believed in miracles, Bernard would be one.

In 1972, at almost 21 years of age, Bernard was finally released from Willowbrook. He is still employed as an advocate for the disabled and lives in his own apartment. I am honored to be one of his friends.

33

LOSS

We lost many lives at Willowbrook, both children and adults. In any large group of people, over a period of time, there will be death. But we knew there were additional factors at Willowbrook: overcrowding, neglect, inadequate food and inadequate medical services. A large number of the residents were profoundly retarded and multiply handicapped. Many, like Lara, were suffering from cerebral palsy, some undiagnosed, and were in the advanced stages of spasticity and joint contractures. These people could not be easily moved and many had difficulty in eating, chewing and swallowing. As a result, many were quite frail and were in great jeopardy. We were struggling to empty the institution into community homes but we were fighting the clock. Every day a resident spent in Willowbrook was a day that resident was disproportionately likely to meet an early death.

Each additional death became a new and unique trauma for me. Each death would give me deep feelings of loss and personal failure. I was particularly affected by two of them. One was the death of a profoundly retarded boy named David. He died as a young teenager while still living at Willowbrook, and he had had a miserable life there. He had lived in an overcrowded, filthy, smelly residence, devoid of decoration or personal items, without adequate or trained staff. His mashed food was force-fed. David was a frail and fragile young man who never had an opportunity to taste, feel or see the beauty of life. He was sentenced to a life in Willowbrook.

David never had the opportunity to leave Willowbrook or the chance to experience life in a real home. He died during the winter months. He was buried in a cemetery located on Staten Island near his parents' home. The day was painfully cold. Fewer than 10 people attended the burial under a gray and frozen sky. I could not help but think that, if we had moved a little faster, opened up a few more community residences, that maybe, just maybe. . .

He might not have a long life but at least he would have lived in a house, sleeping in a bedroom instead of a ward. At least he would have lived with dignity.

I was disappointed, frustrated and angry. I wanted to memorialize him. So I wrote a poem for him and his mother.

I will preface this by saying that my degree is in law, not poetry. My real qualification is "Dad." Also, David's mother appreciated it, so I am sure she would not object. She knows that, though I did not know David well, I loved him, the same way that she loved Lara. We were in this together.

We lost another child today

When will the dying end

When will they turn the prisoners free

When will all humans blend?

We lost another child today

We buried him in the cold

Another child another day

Perhaps he had grown old.

When will we see that lovely day

When children won't be lost

When lives will simply pass away

And the young not suffer most.

(January 1977)

The other case was a young man who lived in Westchester County, New York. I will call him Glenn. He was a sweet, severely to profoundly retarded member of the Willowbrook Class. Someone working for the panel told me about his case. "He's going to die," he said. "His cancer can be treated, but they won't treat it. Nothing can be done."

I investigated Glenn's situation. I spoke to his group home manager and his caseworker.

"His mother's against the treatment. She feels that Glenn has had enough and so has she," said the manager.

"So that's it?" I asked. "He dies?"

"She's his mother!"

"I really love Glenn," the caseworker pleaded. "He is such a sweet man but I could never bear him suffering."

I went to the community residence where Glenn lived. I interviewed the staff, reviewed all the records and spent several hours with Glenn. Certainly, he was severely retarded. He could not speak, and he could only respond to very basic directions. But he seemed happy. I met with his oncologist.

"Yes, he's suffering from a very aggressive cancer which is terminal if not treated. But it may be possible to treat and hopefully cure it."

The first stage of the treatment was a simple process that was minimally invasive. It would determine the likelihood of the cancer being treatable. If it was, the second stage of treatment would be intrusive but would have an 80 percent success rate.

Glenn's mother resided in Florida and would not speak with me. She firmly opposed any treatment. The logic of this escaped me. A chance to save a sweet life was all but irresistible to me. Insurance covered his treatment. She was not visiting Glenn regularly. I only imagined that she would have been happier if she no longer needed to worry about him. Having a profoundly retarded child can challenge you in many ways.

"He is an adult," I argued. "Why should his mother decide whether he lives or dies? Courts should make such determinations."

Since Glenn was a Willowbrook class member, I secured a hearing before Judge Bartels. "Neither Glenn's mother nor any other person was appointed as his guardian," I argued. "He is entitled to have a judge render a decision. He is entitled to have an opportunity to live."

"It's none of your business," shouted one anonymous caller into my phone one morning.

"I am a member of the Willowbrook Review Panel, Glenn is a Willowbrook class member and he is my client. Who is calling, please?" Click.

A hearing was held before Judge Bartels. All relevant witnesses gave sworn testimony: Glenn's mother, the group home manager, the caseworker and the oncologist. At the close of the testimony, Judge Bartels said, "Thank you counsel and, in particular, thank you Mr. Schneps for your devoted and vigorous service on behalf of Glenn but I must support the mother's decision and your application is denied."

I left the courtroom fuming. I was *right!* I was right, and they were wrong.

And as if to drive the point home, the next news I got about the case was that Glenn had died. He had been moved from the residence to a hospital where, by his mother's decree, they withheld treatment, just keeping him comfortable until he died.

I had always admired and respected Judge Bartels. But I would never forgive him for not trying to save Glenn. I was *right* and they were *wrong*.

Except for one thing, I was wrong.

It took me many years to rethink it, even to be willing to rethink it. Many sleepless, troubled nights haunted me before I could contemplate a different perspective. Judge Bartels did not say Glenn should not live. The oncologist did not promise him life. And his mother did not say anything to indicate she did not care about her son. There was no way she could explain a painful series of tests and procedures to a son who did not understand speech. And perhaps she was right. Perhaps that was the best path for her son.

It took decades before I could accept that it was *her* decision, not mine. That was what Judge Bartels ruled. Not that it was a *good or bad* decision. Just that it was *hers*.

And he thanked me. Nice work, counselor. Fight your fights and write your poems. But you do not know what is right for everyone and you do not have the power over life and death. That does not mean that it will not hurt when you cannot save a life.

For some unexplained reason, and despite several hospitalizations while she was at Willowbrook, I had never contemplated that Lara could die before me. That kind of loss was something that happened to other people and something it was my job to prevent.

34

THE PANEL IS DISBANDED

Prior to the enactment of the 1979/1980 annual budget for the State of New York , Mr. James Introne, the new Commissioner for OMRDD leaked the word that he wanted to alter the membership of the Willowbrook Review Panel to have a panel of individuals who were flexible and not ideologues, like Jim Clements, Linda Glenn and Murray Schneps.

Conversations flew over the telephone lines between our old friend Chris Hansen of the NYCLU, and Jim Clements, Linda Glenn, Mike Lottman and me. Apparently, the State did not object to Mike but we were all in the mix and it was decided that we would accept no change of the membership unless we received a commitment to fulfill the obligations of the Consent Judgment. I also believed that Jim Introne enlisted Bruce Ennis, who had represented the plaintiffs in the Willowbrook Class Action, to help him bring in more manageable panel members.

We were unable to make a deal and, not long after, we learned that the New York State Legislature enacted its budget for 1979/1980 eliminating the funding for the Willowbrook Review Panel.

"I guess they really wanted us out," Jim said.

"No question about it," answered Mike.

"What do they really want and what are they willing to give?" Jim asked.

I said, "Well, we're still here now. We're not gonna just walk out the door and let them do whatever they want to do."

Jim said, "We need to communicate with Jim Introne and see what he'll offer."

It was simple; Commissioner Introne wanted permission to open 15 to 50 bed "community residences." 15 to 50 beds was a huge leap. We never wanted more than eight beds. I only wanted three bed units. In addition, he sought a new review panel without Jim Clements or Murray Schneps.

I said, "I'm not happy with us leaving the Panel but that's not the point. I'll never agree to amending the basic provisions of the Judgment."

Chris Hansen said, "Murray, without our consent, they'll do it anyway, or worse!"

"But Chris!" I insisted. "Once we accept those unacceptable conditions, we'll never be able to go back! If we don't agree, we can always re-open the case and fight another day. It's okay to go down fighting but let's not voluntarily surrender!"

I won that argument. We did not sign Commissioner Introne's "devil's bargain" to undo the Consent Judgment. But the Willowbrook Review Panel was disbanded.

Paragraph "2" of the Willowbrook Consent Judgment, the very paragraph that I had objected to years earlier, was held valid. The legislature could refuse to fund the Review Panel without jeopardy to the defendants. On the plus side, Judge Bartels found that conditions at Willowbrook had seriously deteriorated. He appointed a special master to monitor the provisions of the Willowbrook Consent Judgment. However, the special master was without the extraordinary powers held by the Willowbrook Review Panel. Moreover, he was not an ideologue. No formal recommendation power existed.

Upon the termination of the Panel and its formal recommendation authority, the number of community placements slowed to just a trickle and the conditions at Willowbrook deteriorated even further. Shortly thereafter, Chris Hansen prepared and filed a contempt motion against the State for its failure to comply with the provisions of the Willowbrook Consent Judgment.

My days with the Panel were over. It had been quite a run.

PART THREE

35

GOODBYE SWEET GIRL

It was a clear, mild Friday morning in February 1986. February 21st, to be exact. Fourteen years to the day since we had taken Lara out of Willowbrook. The kids were getting ready for school with the excitement and anticipation that goes with Fridays.

We had not yet told them the latest about my defective heart valve or that open-heart surgery to replace the valve had been planned for the following month.

We sat at the kitchen table, eating, talking and planning the weekend. Elizabeth was 15, Samantha was 9, and Joshua was 7. Elizabeth was a glorious teenager planning her sweet 16 party. Samantha was a beautiful, social and loving girl. Joshua had grown to be the boy I wish I had been: caring, happy and with lots of friends.

The kitchen phone rang. I grabbed it. "Hello."

Frequently, Elizabeth beat me to the telephone. But not that time.

At the other end of the line, I heard a hesitant voice. "Mr. Schneps? This is Aaron, the night attendant from the apartment."

Lara's group apartment was just a few blocks from our home.

"What's going on, Aaron?" Vicki caught my eye, with the kind of telepathic link parents share in crisis.

"You should come over. Lara's in trouble."

"What kind of—"

He hung before I could finish.

In minutes Vicki and I got ready, told the kids to stay home with Elizabeth, and were out the door. We pulled up in front of Lara's building and rushed into her apartment. We found her in her bedroom, unresponsive and lying on her back. Although she was nearly 18, she was less than four feet long and only about 40 pounds. She was still like an infant in needs and behavior and slept in a bed with rails. Her thick, dark red hair was tied back in a long ponytail. Her porcelain skin looked so very white. She was still and so cold to the touch. Her favorite Snoopy doll lay beside her and a small mobile hung over her head.

An attendant with a worried look said, "She's not breathing."

"We tried to resuscitate her but it didn't help."

She turned to a pockmarked young man I took for Aaron. They looked at each other knowing what we did not want to face.

I immediately leaned over the side rails. I put my mouth over her mouth and nose and blew hard in and out:

one, two, three, four, five! I pressed her chest rhythmically. I checked her pulse and her heart. Nothing. I leaned over her and kept pressing on her chest, again and again and again. I did not feel tired. I was reviving my child.

I took out my clean handkerchief and handed it to Vicki. She was crying as the EMTs finally charged in and took over. Although we knew she was gone, they attached an automatic breathing pump to her mouth and nose, compressed her chest and rolled her into their ambulance, and it went screaming through the morning streets. They continued to work on her as Vicki held Lara's free hand, saying the things mothers say.

"I love you. I'm right here."

I followed in my car, arriving at the emergency entrance right behind the ambulance. They wheeled her out of the ambulance and into the hospital and through the double doors, working on her all the way, and leaving us feeling frightened and helpless.

We waited.

After 20 minutes, a doctor in scrubs came out.

"Mr. and Mrs. Schneps?" We nodded. "We did everything we could. We couldn't revive her. We're sorry."

He probably gave us some science—told us what they had done, and how, and in what order, and what killed her, and why it was not his fault. All I heard was, "We're sorry. Your daughter is dead."

Vicki cried out, a single gasp, then seemed to catch herself.

We quickly agreed and I asked the doctor, "Can—can any of her organs be used. You know, for anyone else?"

That gave us a sense of perpetuating Lara. She was otherwise healthy. She had no serious illness since leaving Willowbrook.

"Yes. Thank you. We will remove her corneas and then you can be with her to say goodbye." How strange that our blind daughter would enable another person to see.

It was so hard to see our sweet Lara lying in the hospital, so white and so cold. But still, we hugged her and kissed her, just in case part of her was still inside there somewhere, in case she could hear.

I leaned close to her ear. "I love you so much. I will always love you. I will never forget you. I will think of you every day."

Vicki whispered something I did not hear. It was between them. Then she snipped a lock of Lara's red hair and wrapped it in a tissue and made for the door.

We made it to the car, climbed in and slammed the doors. And I heard a low, moaning sound, not a polite lady crying, but crying like a child, a deep, heartfelt grief, from Vicki's heart, from her guts.

And why couldn't I cry like that? Who made that rule?

By the time we got home it was noon. Elizabeth, Samantha and Joshua were dressed and anxiously waiting for us.

One look at our faces and they knew. There were hugs and tears. We held them close. Who knew what fate could take them away? We lost one. Why not two?

For them the loss was confusing. They had lost Lara in parts along the way. Somewhere they had learned she would never see them, never talk to them, never grow up, never cheer at their graduations, never dance at their weddings, and they would never dance at hers. Now she was gone completely. I wondered if it came as a relief. At least we could not lose any more of her.

"Don't let the children come to the funeral," my mother said. "They'll be too sad and upset."

Vicki's mother agreed, "It's not a place for children."

Of course they will be sad, I thought. They are supposed to be sad. But then they get the chance to say goodbye.

Jewish funerals are not held on Saturdays so we buried Lara that Sunday.

As soon as we got home from the hospital we realized that we needed to go to the cemetery where my family is buried and purchase a plot. For Vicki, this was no simple task. We had to *shop*. No space was available next to my family, so they took us to a new area with vacant plots. We selected an eight-plot gravesite situated near a beautifully matured oak tree.

From the time we left from our home to the synagogue for the service and then to the cemetery and back home, I held Vicki, Elizabeth, Samantha and Joshua close.

Goodbye, my sweet girl. You never turned 18; you never got to be a grown-up. But you look so normal right now, like you are sleeping. Maybe now you *are* normal. You can never be hurt, never feel pain, or sadness, or loneliness, or frustration, or a million emotions you did not have the words to express.

We were back at the house after the funeral to begin the *Shiva*. In Jewish tradition, *Shiva* is a period of mourning. Friends and relatives come over and bring food and love, while the family sits and mourns and talks and laughs, and cries.

Unless they are men from Brooklyn.

Everyone was there. My mom in the kitchen telling everyone what to do, and my sister Millie and my brother Herbie, and Vicki's parents there talking to Elizabeth and playing with Samantha and Joshua. And Malachy and Diana, and Chris Hansen, and Michael and Sylvia Lottman, and many other people I could not acknowledge at the funeral.

There is such a thing as strangers and business associates shaking your hand and offering polite condolences. But then there is such a thing as your house filled with nearly everyone you have ever loved, who has ever loved you, and respected you, and argued with you, and fought the good fight, shoulder to shoulder with you. They packed the kitchen and living room, and talked, and ate, and helped to hold us up.

" My son," Malachy said, "yer lookin' a bit green."

"I need some air." I felt my breath getting short and I made my way through the crowd to the front door, smiling at the rug. I was wearing a tweed jacket that seemed like plenty when I hit the winter air and took a few deep breaths. But my breaths kept coming short so I got in the car and drove, and turned and turned and turned and parked and killed the engine.

I look around and I see that I have parked in front of Lara's apartment building.

I started to shake. Am I having a seizure? A heart attack? Should I have had the surgery sooner? My face is twisting and my head is shaking and there is water coming down my cheeks. And I realize that I am crying. Finally.

36

GHOSTS

Barely three weeks after Lara's death, I had open heart surgery. We had set the date well before her death. I considered the possibility of rescheduling. I also considered the possibility of putting my wife and surviving children through a second funeral.

With respect to my heritage, they replaced the faulty valve in my heart with a mechanical one, an artificial mitral heart valve, rather than with one harvested from a pig.

It was March 17, 1986, 14 years to the day after the Willowbrook case was filed. It was also St. Patrick's Day. I told Malachy I had made sure the surgery was handled by a surgeon who was not of Irish lineage.

He beamed. "Don't ye trust us, Muddy?"

"Not on St. Patrick's Day," I laughed.

Needless to say, the surgery was successful and the metal valve continues to perform flawlessly to this day.

September 17, 1987, exactly a year and a half later, I learned the news from Mike Lottman. We spoke only once in a great while, buddies from a forgotten war.

"Did you hear?"

"Hear what?"

"They closed Willowbrook."

Robert Kennedy called it a Snake Pit in 1965. Malachy railed against its depleted staff and conditions on his radio show from 1969 into the early 1970s. Geraldo Rivera exposed it on TV in 1972. The court mandated that it become a facility of no more than 250 people under the Willowbrook Consent Judgment of 1975. We spent 1975 to 1980 trying to carry out that judgment. In 1986, the State announced plans to close it down. I heard the news but, oddly, I did not rejoice. The last "students" were to leave that very day. No more "learning" there.

"Murray? You there?"

"I'm here. What happened?"

"Beats me."

"The truth was I never worried that Willowbrook would become a 250 bed institution. The State could never afford to maintain it."

"Goodbye and good riddance. Will you go see it?"

"Eventually."

Maybe it was the kids, the job, the memories. We talked a little while and made hazy plans to talk again soon. We were still connected. We would always be. But we were connected to the past.

And for all that the years had changed me—the battles, the joys, the losses—I needed to see Willowbrook alone.

A few days later I took the Verrazano Narrows Bridge to the Staten Island Parkway, went to Victory Boulevard into the grounds of Willowbrook and parked. The parking lot was nearly empty. A few random workers were there, presumably emptying files, taking surveys, locking up. I saw the brick building with the two outside staircases ascending in an inverted "V," where Vicki and I had been startled by the friendly retarded man and his mild disability was enough to frighten us. The five "baby buildings" that fanned out around the "therapy center" where Lara had been promised various types of therapy. And the infamous Building 6 where, on a cold and windy morning in January 1972, Mike Wilkins introduced Geraldo Rivera to the reality that was Willowbrook.

I could almost see the affidavit I had written for the Willowbrook Class Action before me and remember how I viewed my role back in 1972, but now I was able to view my affidavit within the perspective of time and circumstances. In those early years I had conflicted feelings, desires, needs and pressures. My perceptions were, necessarily, myopic.

I knew I wanted more children after Lara, *normal* children, much as it hurt to say she was not normal. I would have had a sad and diminished life if I had not had the children who followed Lara.

But Lara should have been my first through tenth priority. While I was able to present serious and compelling reasons as to why Lara was institutionalized in Willowbrook, the truth of the matter is that we agreed to place Lara in Willowbrook in spite of the fact that we had to know she would have less of a life there than she would with us. Of course, Lara's mental and physical disabilities would not have improved if she lived at home, but she would have been with us on a daily basis. This would have been a great and incalculable benefit to her. Removing her from our home and forcing her to live in a cave like Willowbrook, changed her life. In spite of the fact that I loved her, I set aside everything that I knew about being a father and protector of my own child and permitted her to move from our home, her home, to an alien and cold large State institutional residential facility.

It was clear that the chances of Lara approaching normalcy, or even progressing in any real manner were nil. She would always be profoundly retarded, blind, unable to speak, unable to feed herself, dress herself, sit by herself, ambulate, or do anything on her own. She would always need full-time assistance. Vicki's cockeyed optimism was not going to change that. Yet we could have made her more comfortable. She could have slept in her own room on her own bed, sat on soft, clean carpets, and been cuddled and sung to daily by people who loved her.

This is my shame. Perhaps that shame fueled me to fight for the rights of Lara and other mentally retarded institutionalized people. Had I applied that energy to Lara, if had we used our time and energy to raise Lara in our home, she would have had a better life. Perhaps - others would have lost out.

And whether my other children would have been born is a serious but unanswerable question.

At least I had the sense and the resources to take her out of that hellhole when I was able to see just how bad it was. Not so for David's mother, Rosalie. David died there of neglect, along with uncounted other Davids over the decades. When the Willowbrook case was filed in 1972, there were 5,700 residents living here. As of April 1982, 1108 had been placed into community residences, 580 were placed into family care (a situation where a family accepts a handicapped person to reside with them in their home or apartment), 730 were discharged and 557 had died. I stood before the empty looming buildings. They looked far more like a prison complex than a school. Like Andersonville and Elmira, where Civil War prisoners were held until starvation or disease took them away. Or in the cleaner wards, where they were simply confined, given little of the promised therapy or education or attention that was supposed to encourage their souls.

And here the buildings stood, empty and silent. As I walked around I was overcome with sadness. So many people, so many children had suffered here for so long. I did not feel elated that it was closing. I felt like it had taken too long, like I had somehow failed to close it sooner. Too many suffered, too many died to feel victorious.

On the way back I bypassed my own house and drove on to Little Neck, to Gaskel Road and the group home there, the site of one of our first great triumphs. It still stood and flourished. I pulled up in front. It was a dark brown Tudor home with a roof with Spanish tiles. It had a large covered entrance with several steps up from the walk and a large window on each side of the entrance. Three small windows were on the second story.

I drove to the front of the house, turned off my car and sat for a while, just thinking. After a few minutes, I went to the front door and rang the bell.

A female attendant greeted me at the door with a smile, a good sign.

Why was I here? What should I say? What did I really want?

"I'm...I'm Murray Schneps."

"Yes?"

"I was involved in opening this group home, would it be okay if I walk around outside for a little while?

"Sure, you can walk around. Would you like to come in?"

"No, thanks, I just want to walk around a bit. Excuse me, are any of the children at home?"

"No, they are all at their day programs and will not be at home for a couple of hours. I am preparing dinner for them."

"Thank you for your letting me walk around."

I walked around the side of the house. There was an ample grass back yard for the children to play and relax. The weather was good for outdoor playing. I slowly panned the back yard and remembered the battles to open this first home. From the outside this looked just like any other house inhabited by a family. And it was.

I thought about hanging around to welcome the children as they returned home from school and talk to them and play with them. But I had seen what I wanted to see and it was time for me to leave. Perhaps, I would return another time. For now it was enough to confirm the existence of the group home I had helped create.

I again knocked on the door and thanked the attendant for her cooperation and help.

"Have a great day and thanks for all you do for the children. Goodbye."

At one time, Vicki and I had fantasized that our Lara would live in that group home. Perhaps in some ways she did.

37

A FEW WORDS TO NEW PARENTS

I wish to offer a few thoughts for you to consider. It is my hope that some of the following words will assist you and ease your journey:

1. Welcome to the new reality in your life.

2. Of course, you will always love your child but it's OK to acknowledge that it is a raw deal for them and for you. It isn't fair but you cannot let yourself get stuck.

3. Many services and facilities, as well as funds, are available to assist your handicapped child. You are not alone.

4. Obtain an accurate assessment of your child's disabilities and needs and embark on a life long quest for information on how to meet those needs.

5. Never blindly accept advice you do not understand, especially if it makes no sense or seems wrong for your child.

6. Do everything within your power to keep your child at home with you and your family and make persistent efforts to secure and maintain the necessary programs, services and funding. But if your child's needs can only be met in a small community residential facility then accept that reality.

7. Tell your other children the truth and permit them to help. This is a family project.

8. Do not try to be a martyr by doing it all yourself. Get as much help as you can, so that you and your family will have as normal a life as is possible.

9. The vast majority of handicapped children will improve with appropriate nurturing and services. But there is no standard developmental curve for handicapped children, so do not expect your child to fit into a predictable process.

10. Be politically aware and get to know your politicians. Educate your politicians so they understand that the handicapped citizen in your family is part of their constituency and that you expect them to support funding to maintain services for the handicapped.

11. The fight will never end as long as your child is alive, no matter how excellent things may be at any one time. Changes in the economy and the political atmosphere can easily diminish services and support networks.

12. The quality and amount of services, support systems and financial aid may vary greatly from state to state and even within a particular state. Some may consider moving to a different state, or to a different jurisdiction within a state, to obtain better services.

13. Keep in mind that the voluntary agencies, who provide services for the handicapped and rely upon State and Federal funding, cannot be proper advocates. They have an inherent conflict of interest and the larger the voluntary agency, the larger the conflict of interest.

Good luck my friends. I will be praying for all of you and your children.

EPILOGUE

On May 23, 1968, the day my daughter Lara Rebecca Schneps was born, I was 30 years of age; on May 5, 1975, the day the Willowbrook Consent Judgment was executed, I was 37; on February 21, 1986, the day Lara died, I was 48. This book is about those nearly 18 years, a lifetime for Lara and a life-altering time for me. For many years friends urged me to write a book about my experiences around the Willowbrook State School. The prospect frightened me. First, because it was so important. Even a subjective discussion of Willowbrook and our struggles on the Panel had to be good, really good, a manifesto. And also because it would revolve around Lara. Outside of our immediate circle, if anyone remembered her they would remember her from my book.

I put it off.

Then, in September 1995, I suffered my first stroke. I seemed to completely recover, except that I flipped pronouns, a condition referred to as pronoun aphasia. I said "him" when I meant "her," "he" when I meant "she" and so forth. I made a simple adjustment: I stopped using pronouns and would only use proper names in court. "Mister Smith was under the impression that…" People got to hear their names more often than they were accustomed but no one complained.

In January 2005, I suffered what we thought was my second stroke. We learned that I had had a previous but undetected stroke. So, in 2005 I suffered my third stroke and it took much from me. I was left unable to read or write effectively. Curiously, my abilities to do math and to use a plethora of curse words were unaffected. The gang from Brighton Beach would have been proud.

Recovery was a long struggle. Even now, I can only comprehend one voice at a time, so group discussions can be difficult. One-to-one discussions work best. I can read and write, but not the way I once could. I cannot enjoy foreign movies with English subtitles. If a subtitle has more than four words, I cannot read or comprehend it fast enough.

But again several friends urged me to write this book. Almost 40 years and three strokes after Lara's birth, I felt the moment was ripe. I told them I would do it. Then I told my family I was going to do it. I even told some casual acquaintances I was doing it. All this was to make sure I would be too embarrassed to back out. I stopped worrying about writing a great book. I no longer had the skills. Any book would be an accomplishment. At least my children and grandchildren would know who Lara was and what I had done. I just wanted it written.

As I look over these pages, I can see something about who I was at 31, beginning a life so different from the one I had planned, and who I became over the next 18 years, following the path on which Lara launched me. In spite of my advocacy and my love for Lara, the notion of being handicapped was at a distance, like the mildly retarded man at the top of the stairs whose very presence made Vicki and me run away. After my third stroke, I could see that I, too, was handicapped. I was not reaching down. People had to help me. I reached up. And I was grateful.

This is part of my story.

With the passing of time, I no longer fight on the front lines and do not want to be involved in any more wars. However, I can reflect and recognize that I loved and admired Jim Clements, Mike Lottman, Linda Glenn, Chris Hansen, and Bill Bitner. They were great friends and honorable people. Sadly, Jim and Bill have passed. I wish I could thank them personally. But I know that energy can never be destroyed, only converted into another form of energy. I often wonder what Jim and Bill's energy is up to right now.

In spite of the fact that we were not 100% successful, I achieved my own specific goals. I had vowed to protect Lara, to close Willowbrook and to create three-bed community residences. And I did it, not alone of course but those goals were achieved.

Still, I have never forgotten my interview with Robert Keating for his article, "The War Against the Mentally Retarded," that appeared in New York Magazine on September 17, 1979:

> It's a battle. If we're going to take advantage of the opportunity given to us by the Willowbrook decree, if we're going to make it so people no longer have to be destroyed in institutions, then we can't be chickening out because some nut burns a house down.

If it doesn't work here, it won't work anywhere. No place else has the decree that we have. Nor a review panel with the power this one has. And no place in the country is funded the way this case is. It can't be all wasted because of prejudice.

New York has a tremendous responsibility – if we fail here, we fail for everybody. No one's going to have a chance for another 50 years. It'll be back to those damn institutions.

Despite the passage of over 30 years, my concerns remain unabated.

Even though it was frustrating to have the Panel's work prematurely discontinued before finish our job and close Willowbrook, we made significant headway. In 1975, 20,062 mentally retarded individuals resided in New York State owned and operated institutions. As of September 30, 2011, there were only 1,228 mentally retarded individuals living in just nine New York State institutions. None of them live in Willowbrook or Suffolk. And many other States have been following the lead of the Willowbrook Consent Judgment. New York State loves to take the credit for the dismantling the institutional system, which it did but only after many years of prodding and pushing.

In order to be safe from another movement (which I have a terrible feeling will come) to open and operate institutions, it is necessary to raze or otherwise render such buildings unavailable or incapable of being utilized as institutions. The only viable solution is to flatten all the Willowbrooks once and for all.

Perhaps the State will move forward and finally close its remaining residential institutions. In a letter I received from Commissioner Courtney Burke of the New York State Office for People With Developmental Disabilities, formerly the Office of Mental Retardation and Developmental Disabilities, dated September 6, 2011, she stated:

we are committed to achieve closure of
all developmental centers by the end of 2014.

I hope she keeps her promise. The advocates and families of the mentally retarded must never drop their guard. Danger always lurks. While my story ends, the story of so many will go on. We must all be forever vigilant.

Sometimes late at night, this project—this book that let me spend every day with Lara again—almost done, I walk down the hall in my robe and slippers, still taking care not to make noise, as if I were afraid of waking Elizabeth, Samantha, and Joshua, as if they were not already grown and moved away, raising children of their own. I scan photos of me and my loved ones: me as a tough kid in Brighton Beach, as a ball player, as a freshly minted lawyer, as a new dad, as an advocate, as a dad again. As I see who I was then, I reflect on who I am now, retired tough guy, retired lawyer, retired warrior.

Retired dad? Never! Not since Lara fought her way into the world and selected me as her dad.

I look at the last picture on the wall, the faded photo of Lara and me taken on a sunny Spring day in 1975. I am singing to her, she is smiling, joyful, Lara exuding love. We both seem to be in a private place, just her and me. I see you my sweet girl.

It doesn't matter where you are
I can see how fair you are
I close my eyes and there you are always

END

WILLOWBROOK IMAGES[2]

---

[2] These photographs, placed into evidence during the Willowbrook Class Action (NYSARC and Parisi v. Rockefeller, 72 Civil 356, 357), were released by the Order of Judge Raymond J. Dearie of the United States District Court, Eastern District of New York, dated April 1, 2014. Such permission was mandated by the prior Order of Judge Orrin G. Judd of the United States District Court, Eastern District of New York, dated July 12, 1972.

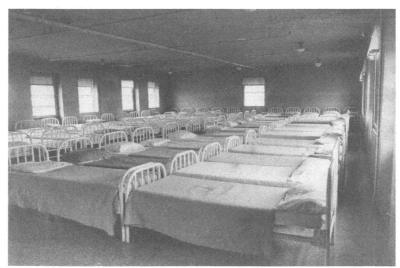

Empty ward – adults

Man restrained in a chair

Empty ward - children

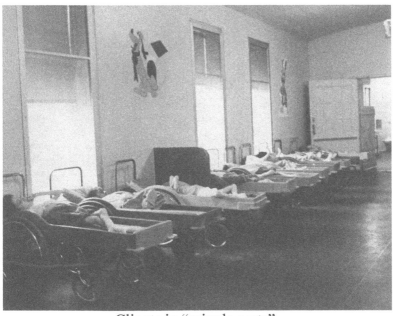

Clients in "cripple carts"

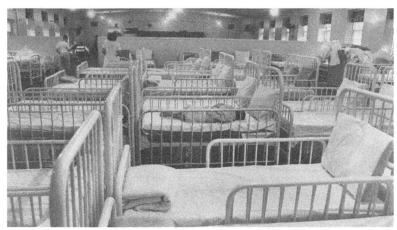

Empty ward – baby building

Children lying on mats

Boy sleeping on terrazzo floor

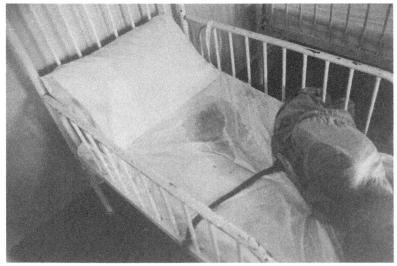

Child restrained in urine soaked bed

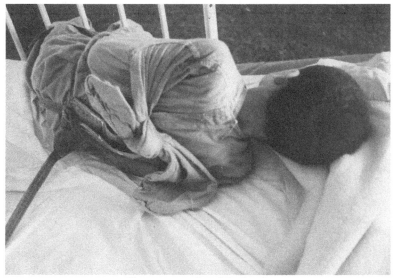

Boy restrained in bed

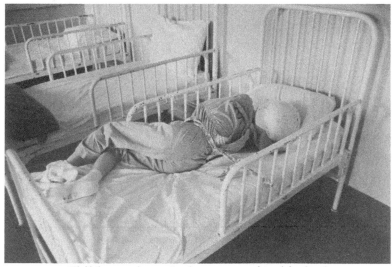

Child wearing a helmet restrained in bed

Idleness in a dayroom

Boys in stages of undress sitting in idleness

Girls with multiple injuries

Boy squatting alone at the radiator

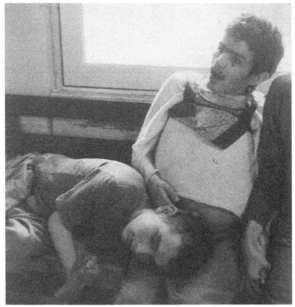

Boys sitting together

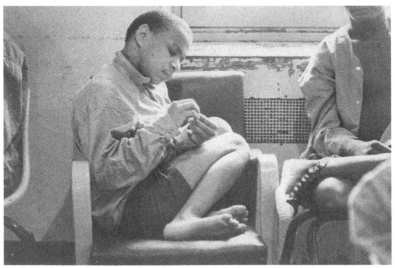

Boy sitting in front of the radiator